RESTAURANT

MARKETING FOR OWNERS AND MANAGERS

Patti J. Shock

John T. Bowen

John M. Stefanelli

WILEY

JOHN WILEY & SONS, INC.

Published by John Wiley & Sons, Inc., Hoboken, New Jersey

Published simultaneously in Canada

For general information on our other products and services or for technical support, please contact our Customer Care Department within the United States at (800) 762-2974, outside the United States at (317) 572-3993 or fax (317) 572-4002.

Wiley also publishes its books in a variety of electronic formats. Some content that appears in print may not be available in electronic books. For more information about Wiley products, visit our web site at www.wiley.com.

Library of Congress Cataloging-in-Publication Data:

Shock, Patti J.
    Restaurant marketing for owners and managers / Patti J. Shock, John T. Bowen, John M. Stefanelli.
        p. cm. — (Wiley restaurant basics series)
    Includes index.
    ISBN 0-471-22627-0
        1. Restaurants—Marketing.   2. Food service management.   I. Bowen, John T.
    II. Stefanelli, John M.   III. Title.   IV. Series.

TX911.3.M3 S55 2004
647.795'068'8—dc21

2002155597

Printed in the United States of America

10   9   8   7   6   5   4   3   2   1

CONTENTS

PREFACE

Like most long-term projects, this one started out simple enough: with a question.

John Stefanelli was chatting with a restaurant company's management recruiter about three years ago. This active recruiter wondered why most graduates of hospitality management programs knew a lot about food and service, but very little about beverage operations and marketing. She commented further that, while the UNLV graduates she interviews are adequately prepared in beverage operations, still they lacked restaurant marketing and food merchandising skills.

When John mentioned this to Patti Shock, she suggested developing a restaurant marketing elective course. After conducting this course, however, it became very clear to her that, although there was a need in academia for this type of curriculum, it seemed as if the greater need was in the restaurant community—specifically, among independent restaurant owners and managers.

Patti became more deeply interested in this issue. She started looking around for written materials and Internet sites that focused on restaurant marketing, particularly marketing for the independent restaurant operator. She concluded that there is a wealth of material out there, but a great deal of it is academic, and therefore not suitable for the typical restaurant operator. Furthermore, there doesn't appear to be an all-encompassing source, one that pulls together all of the critical elements into one organized package.

So, in her usual enthusiastic way, Patti cornered John Stefanelli and John Bowen and wouldn't let them go until they agreed to help her develop this package. You have the result in your hand.

This package is somewhat unusual. It doesn't contain charts, pictures, sidebars, colors, or graphics. Its layouts don't look like those in *USA Today* and other contemporary resources, though there is plenty of that in the unique companion Web site to this book, which Patti maintains and revises regularly (http://tca.unlv.edu/profit). This book just has words. It's intended to be a conversation. As you read it, visualize the four of us sitting together, enjoying an entertaining, informative, interactive experience.

Let us stress that we welcome the opportunity to interact with you. We don't want this to be a one-way communication. No one book can ever claim to be the last word on any subject. We believe that this book and its accompanying Web site provide a thorough view of restaurant marketing for owners and managers, as well as an almost endless list of marketing and merchandising ideas that you can use right now to enhance your bottom line. However, because books and Web sites reflect real life, they are subject to revision and alteration as the restaurant industry grows and changes. Therefore, we need your suggestions and ideas. Patti is especially eager to incorporate reader feedback into the book's Web site. In that way, we can share information and together contribute to the betterment of our industry and our way of life.

The three of us bring a unique combination of experiences and education to the table. We are all approaching our "golden years"; between us, we have over 120 years of restaurant/hospitality experience, both in the trenches as well as in the classrooms and laboratories of major universities. Each of us has written books, articles, newspaper/magazine stories, and the like. John Bowen has written marketing columns for trade magazines. Patti Shock has been the keynote speaker for many marketing and marketing-related conferences/seminars/workshops. And John Stefanelli supervised the William F. Harrah College of Hotel Administration's restaurant and catering facilities for several years. We think we know what it takes to run a restaurant and fill the room with happy, paying customers—but we'll let you be the judge of that.

It took a lot of people a lot of time to put this package together. We had a great deal of help along the way, and we would like to thank everyone who contributed his or her time and energy. We especially want to thank the following reviewers: Bill Allen, Rob Grimes, Stephen Michaelides, Jim Moore, and Larry Ross.

But that's enough talk for now. Ready, set, market!

Patti Shock
John Bowen
John Stefanelli

1

INTRODUCTION: WHAT AM I GETTING MYSELF INTO?

Marketing is everything the customer sees,
touches, hears, or smells.
Jim Moore, Founder and Leader, Moore Ideas, Inc.

Marketing gives life to your restaurant. Well-planned and -executed marketing will bring customers to your restaurant. And it will bring them back. It will help keep them happy. And you'll be pretty happy, too.

Although this book is written for owners and managers, restaurant marketing is the job of all restaurant employees. An owner or manager must get excited about marketing and transfer that excitement to the staff. Everyone must be engaged every day in your restaurant's marketing efforts.

The essence of marketing is creating an experience that delivers exceptional value to your target market and communicates this message to the target market and your employees.

Successful restaurant owners and managers share a common trait: they are customer focused and strongly committed to marketing.

Due to its dynamic nature, marketing is always exciting and challenging. The marketing plan that creates maximum value for your customers today will not necessarily be the one that does this two years down the road. Your customers are forever changing. You must change with them.

WHY SHOULD YOU READ THIS BOOK?

In 1971, the National Restaurant Association (NRA) published the book, *How to Promote Your Restaurant,* which comments, "The most under-promoted product in America today is the restaurant meal." Things have certainly changed since then.

At that time, independently owned and operated restaurants ruled the restaurant landscape. They sold most of the meals eaten away from home. Today, big restaurant chains have displaced them. The entry of corporate giants into the restaurant industry has transformed it from a mom-and-pop industry into an industry dominated by large chains, in which fewer than 25 companies account for over one-third of restaurant sales in this country. If you are working for one of these conglomerates, you have the edge. If you aren't part of any of these organizations, read on.

Marketing was an option in 1971. Today, it is essential to gaining and keeping a competitive edge. You must use marketing to attract customers, give them a good experience, and capture their future dining business. To do this, you must understand your customers and create a marketing mix that provides value for your target market.

To illustrate how competitive the restaurant industry has become, our research shows that when customers give a restaurant an excellent rating, 80 percent say they will return. However, only 40 percent of those who give it a good rating actually plan to return.

Today, it's not enough to be good. You have to be excellent. Recall the last time you went to a restaurant. When you left, did you say, "It was good"? If so, you're probably not thinking about going back anytime soon. Why should you? In most communities, there are many good restaurants. On the other hand, if you left and said, "That was excellent," not only are you likely to return, you will probably tell others about the great time you had.

Reading about and applying the ideas presented in this book will help you achieve those excellent ratings. You will also be more successful in attracting customers. If you can look up most times of the day and see a waiting line for a table in your restaurant, then we've done an excellent job.

The two dozen or so gigantic restaurant chains operate in a highly competitive environment, where aggressive marketing skills are needed to win customers. They employ corporate directors of marketing who work with advertising agencies and public relations firms. They spend millions of dollars on marketing. If they sneeze, we independent operators catch a cold.

Earth to restaurant owners and managers: This is your competition. Many independent operators and small chains do not have these kinds of marketing resources. Managers of these operations have to use their resources more effectively. This book will show you how to do that.

According to management guru Peter Drucker in *Business Week,* "Marketing encompasses the entire business. It is the whole business seen from the point of view of the customer. Without an understanding of marketing, you do not have a good understanding of business." This book is designed to help you understand and use marketing to increase the profitability of your restaurant.

This is not a textbook. It is more along the lines of what some people refer to as a "self-help" book. It's intended to pass along some good ideas—things you can use right now to make a difference. It's also intended to excite and motivate you.

We intend this book to be accessible. It is written in a conversational manner and is filled with examples of the ways in which other restaurants are using the marketing mix. In order to preserve the flow of this conversation, the book does not contain figures, sample menus, copies of advertisements, or photos.

We are fortunate to have an Internet expert on our team. Patti has won national awards for the development of informational Web sites. She developed and maintains a companion Web site for this book. Instead of showing a black-and-white copy of a year-old menu reduced to illegibility in the book, the Web site offers currently used, full-color menus. The Web site also includes advertisements, promotions, examples of publicity, and other sources that will assist you in developing your marketing mix.

This book will start you on your journey to maximizing the value created by your marketing mix. The Web site will help you to continue that journey.

THE SEVEN Ps OF MARKETING

Marketing involves managing the **marketing mix,** which consists of the seven Ps:

MARKETING MIX Price, product, promotion, place, process, participants, physical evidence.

- *Price:* This is the dollar amount you place on your products. When combined with the other Ps, it denotes a certain value. This value should be consistent with the perceived value the target market places on your products.

- *Product:* This includes your menu items and the other products and services that you buy, prepare, and sell.

- *Promotion:* This is the overall message you relay to your target market, including advertising, sales promotions, personal selling, and public relations efforts.

- *Place:* This includes the location of your restaurant, the surrounding neighborhood, and its accessibility and visibility.

- *Process:* This consists of the way in which you deliver your service. Do you have a buffet? Do your customers get their own soft drinks? How do you handle take-out orders? Do you place the wine jug on the table and let the customers pour their own?

- *Participants:* These are the people you want to participate in your operation. You choose them. They are your customers, employees, and other stakeholders, such as purveyors and other outside service providers.

- *Physical evidence:* Your physical facilities create a particular atmosphere. They provide tangible clues to the customer. For instance, the exterior appearance of Bennigan's lets people know it is a casual restaurant. A neat and clean dining room gives the customer evidence that the restaurant is well managed.

The first four are the traditional Ps, developed for marketing tangible products, such as washing machines and underwear. The other three are unique to restaurants.

Managers often think of marketing and advertising as the same thing. However, advertising is just one form of promotion, which in turn is just one element of the marketing mix. And, depending upon the situation, you may not even use advertising in your mix. For example, some restaurant managers may do an excellent job of crafting the other elements of the marketing mix to create value for their customers. After being in business for several years, the positive word of mouth from customers replaces their paid advertising. In order to maximize the benefits you receive from marketing, you need to understand and use all seven elements of the marketing mix.

Just as you do with ingredients in a menu item, you must determine how you will use the seven Ps as ingredients in your marketing plan. They are interrelated. For example, the mix needed for a successful quick-service restaurant will differ significantly from the one used by an upscale steak house.

Charley Brown's Steak and Lobster opened its first unit in 1965. The concept had seven unique features: display cooking, gaslights, waitress uniforms with short skirts and push-up bras, water view, USDA Prime steaks, signature liquor service and glassware, and sourdough bread flown in daily from San Francisco. Eventually, six of these unique attributes were copied by competitors (all except the water view)—but it took them several years to do it.

This book will help you develop the right marketing recipe. It will give you the tools needed to create a successful mix for your restaurant and will help you create something unique, something that sets you apart from your competition. However, it will also suggest ways to go beyond simply offering a different experience for your guests.

Differentiation is important, but sooner or later your innovations can be copied by your competition—though by that time you'll be on to something else, right? The key is to latch on to a differentiation strategy that renders you unique. It is impossible to copy uniqueness.

CREATING VALUE FOR THE GUEST

Ray Kroc, the founder of McDonald's, created value for the family market with his formula of quality, service, cleanliness, and low-priced food. He referred to his low prices as value and his formula for success as Q, S, C, and V. In the case of McDonald's, value was related to low price. But value does not always mean low price.

Instead of thinking about value, you might want to focus on **perceived value.** It is critical to get inside the customer's mind, to uncover his or her definition of "value" or "great value" or "mediocre value," and so on. It's not what we think, but what customers think that will make the difference. For instance, customers typically perceive a greater value if the quality of the products you sell and the services you provide are attractive and the prices are reasonable. But the perceived value would tend to decline if your prices are thought to be excessive. You will need to play around with the elements of quality, service, and price to develop the best possible combination that will exceed your guests' expectations. In the end, you want your customers to say, "I got my money's worth." If they say that, they'll be back. And they'll make sure other people know about your restaurant.

As Chapter 6 notes, when pricing a product, guests will tend to consider the product's quality and the service provided, along with the price you're charging. These things are generally uppermost in your mind when you're wracking your brain to come up with the appropriate price points.

> **PERCEIVED VALUE** Perceived value is directly related to perceived quality of the goods and services you provide, but is indirectly related to the prices you charge.

But when looking at the big picture, when viewing your operation as one of many restaurants in the community, you should consider other tangible and intangible benefits you can offer that may attract guests and cause them to view value in a different light.

For instance, some guests may be attracted to your operation because of its unique atmosphere, the convenience of valet parking, or the extended hours of operation. Some may fall in love with your willingness to prepare off-menu items. The list of possibilities is endless. All these things can create value. The trick is to find out what they are and how much customers are willing to pay for them.

Although you know that customers will pay for these elements of value, you cannot put a price tag on them unless you take the time to research your customers' needs and desires. For example, chatting with your steady customers may lead you to conclude that most of them have more money than time. Waiting is a cost that can reduce value. Some customers will not wait more than 30 minutes; to them, this wait reduces the value of their experience in your restaurant.

Some restaurants have only one location. The value of the restaurant is reduced as the drive time lengthens. What to do? Often, you can reshuffle the entire marketing mix to create more value, but in this situation there are fewer options. An excellent solution is the Outback Steakhouse **call-ahead program.** This program allows guests to call the restaurant and put their names on the waiting list before they start out on their trip. This reduces the wait time, which creates more value.

CALL-AHEAD PROGRAM This program allows guests to call the restaurant and put their names on the waiting list before they start out on their trip. This reduces the wait time, which creates more value.

Another way to create value is to be different. Provide something no one else has. In today's society, *boring* is bad for your financial health.

A tried-and-true technique used to create value is to put a new spin on an old product. McDonald's differentiated itself by creating a national chain that was clean and offered a consistent product. Burger King differentiated its restaurants from McDonald's by flame-broiling the product, thereby adding value for some customers. Wendy's differentiated itself by adding a number of unique features, such as using fresh hamburgers instead of frozen ones, providing tables with nonattached chairs, and including other similar features that appealed to, and thus created value for, adults. In these ways, each of these quick-service hamburger restaurants differentiated itself and gained a competitive edge.

THOUGHT FOR TODAY

Differentiation is a journey toward uniqueness. It requires considerable dedication. Providing customers with what they value and doing this better than the competition creates excellence.

The service delivered by your employees is a very important element of value. It is also an area where you can distinguish yourself. If you do it well and do it consistently, you will also differentiate yourself and stand out from the crowd.

To be successful at marketing, you must create a service culture in your organization. Your culture should be focused on serving and satisfying your customers. All employees should embrace this culture, which means you must recognize and reward employees who help create value for your customers.

In *Service Management and Marketing*, Christian Gronroos relates a comment from Roger Dow, Marriott's vice president of sales and marketing services: "We used to reward restaurant managers for things that were important to us, such as food costs. When have you heard a customer ask for the restaurant's food costs? You have to reward for what customers want from your business." Today, measuring and rewarding customer satisfaction is part of Marriott's reward system.

> **MARKETING CONCEPT** This consists of customer orientation, integrating marketing throughout the organization, and meeting company objectives.

All in all, in order to provide excellent, consistent value to your guests, you need to adopt the **marketing concept.** This concept consists of three parts:

1. Everyone in the operation must be customer oriented. Restaurants sell service; supermarkets sell food.

2. Marketing must be integrated throughout the organization. Everyone must embrace marketing and its concomitant customer orientation.

3. You must meet company objectives. Roger Dow is not suggesting that we shouldn't be concerned about costs. However, managing costs, producing profits, and creating and maintaining customer counts are equally important. If you create temporary profits by reducing customer value, you will eventually see a steady decline in cover counts and profits.

When creating customer value, you need to add benefits that are worth more to customers than what it costs you to create them. These benefits don't have to be overly elaborate or expensive. A benefit might be something simple, such as putting a special sauce on a grilled salmon dish, making it a house special, and charging $2 more for the item. It might involve developing a specialty dessert at a cost of 75 cents and selling it for $5. Or it might mean developing a service delivery system that reduces your costs but does not reduce customer value.

Good marketing is not an expense. It is an investment. It will generate excitement, enthusiasm, and electricity. It will pay for itself many times over.

Let's get started.

THINGS TO DO TODAY

- Familiarize yourself with this book's Web site. You'll want to visit it often.

- Just for fun, brainstorm with your staff ways to differentiate one of your current menu items, giving it an unusual and unique twist.

- Locate a copy of the NRA's book *How to Promote Your Restaurant*. It will give you a good idea of what restaurant marketing was like 30-some years ago. Read it before you read the rest of this book.

2

LOCATION: WHERE AM I GOING TO PUT THIS PLACE?

Locations are what you make them. There are very few can't-miss, killer locations, just as there are few can't-make-it, loser spots. Most fall somewhere in between. And like most other things in the restaurant industry, a location's success is greatly influenced by the personal skills a manager or owner/manager apply to the restaurant's day-to-day operations.

Likewise, there are very few jinxed locations. Just because several prior occupants of a restaurant location couldn't survive doesn't necessarily mean that someone with the right combination of menu, service, and personal attention can't make it fly.

A lot of things can jinx a location. It could be in an area where there is just too much competition. It might be in a sparsely populated neighborhood. Or the building itself could be suffering from old age and neglect.

A truly jinxed location, though, is usually one with excessive fixed costs; no matter how well you do, you just can't make a go of it. This brings us to the very first thing you should look at when checking out a location: its rent.

RENT

Rent is one of the most critical expenses in the restaurant budget. It's a fixed cost and it is one that will stay with you for some time, usually five years or more. Although you usually have some flexibility with other expenses, you can't do anything about rent except pay it on time.

If you pay a mortgage instead of rent, you can usually afford to sacrifice some profit along the way because, if someday you decide to close the restaurant, you will at least have the real estate that can be sold, thereby making up for some of the profit you lost during the preceding years. It's analogous to a Major League Baseball team that loses money every year but generates a huge capital gain when it's sold. However, since few independent restaurant operators own the property outright, this option generally does not come into play.

If rent payments are too high, you may not lose money, but you'll never make a fair profit. You'll just make the landlord rich. Getting stuck in a situation like this is equivalent to a football team always starting its offense on the five-yard line.

What's too high in rents? Although this is a matter of opinion, experience tells us that if the rent expense exceeds approximately 6 percent of your sales revenue, you're paying too much. For instance, if your rent is $6,000 a month, you should generate sales revenue of approximately $100,000 a month.

When first considering whether the location can generate adequate sales revenue, it's not necessary to do a full-blown analysis. It's better to rely on your experience and knowledge to guide your initial thinking. Ask yourself a couple of things. First, what is the most likely average check that your type of restaurant business would achieve at that location? And second, how many customers per day are you most likely to serve? When you multiply these two figures, and then extend them to one month's worth of sales revenue, you will have a pretty good idea of what's possible.

Let's say you have a quick-service operation and the expected average check is $7. If you're open every day of the month, you will need approximately 475 customers per day at an average check of $7 to achieve monthly sales revenue of $100,000. Take a deep breath and ask yourself if there truly is the potential for attracting that many customers, and, if so, can you serve them adequately? Is it a logical proposition? Based on your experience, does it make sense to proceed? Is the place big enough to accommodate the potential traffic? Is there enough parking? Is the drive-through convenient? You get the idea.

If, after some careful soul-searching, you don't think you can do that much, it's best to pass on the location. It's easy to kid yourself into believing you can generate a high sales revenue. Don't fall into that trap. It's wise to be conservative at this stage.

You might believe that it would be acceptable to pay more than six percent rent because you could reduce other expenses to compensate. Be very careful when walking down this road, as it is easy to fool yourself into thinking that you can beat the odds. A higher rent expense might be feasible if, for example, the landlord takes care of some other expenses for you, such as maintaining the rest rooms in the shopping center, paying the water and sewer bill, or underwriting all the advertising. In other cases, you might be able to afford more rent if your sales revenue includes an above-average proportion of high-profit items, such as merchandise sales (e.g., logo caps and jackets), vending machine income (e.g., video games), or sales of alcoholic beverages.

If you think that you can comfortably afford the rent, check out other related occupancy charges that the landlord expects you to pay. For instance, retail tenants are usually expected to pay for property insurance. They also may have to pay for all repairs and maintenance for the facility. And, if the location is inside a shopping mall, all tenants must usually contribute to a common area maintenance (CAM) fund that is used to maintain the parking lots, repair or replace the roof, and so forth.

These are the kinds of things that are inserted into leases and that might be overlooked when you are considering a particular location. At first glance, you may not think they will amount to too much money. However, a landlord might charge a lower rent and try to make it up with related charges. For instance, if some of the CAM fund is used to pay the water and sewer bills for the entire shopping mall, you may not want to be part of this arrangement if there are several water-guzzler tenants, such as hair and beauty salons, at that location.

"KNOCKOUT" LOCATION CRITERION Anything, such as excessive rent, that forces you to abandon the site.

Rent is a deal breaker. It's a **"knockout" location criterion**. Be careful when making your decision about affordable rent.

INITIAL CASH OUTLAY

If you can't make enough money to pay the rent, there is nothing left to consider—it's time to move on to the next potential location. But if the rent seems reasonable and affordable, the very next knockout criterion you need to consider is the amount of money you must provide up front in order to open the restaurant.

INITIAL CASH OUTLAY Initial investment.

The amount of **initial cash outlay** (sometimes referred to as the *initial investment*) will vary. The type of operation is a key variable; fancier places will cost more to open. Other factors, though, can be just as influential. For instance, the initial cash outlay will probably be higher if you are opening a new property as opposed to converting a prior restaurant or retail business.

It is important to compute the total amount of cash that needs to be invested in order to turnkey the operation—that is, open the doors for business. You must know this figure so that you can determine whether you are able to raise sufficient cash. Just as critical, however, is the need for you to have an accurate figure to compare to the amount of profit you think the restaurant location can generate.

The total initial cash outlay usually includes the following items:

1. Costs of investigating and evaluating potential locations
2. Down payment(s) or purchase price(s) for equipment, furniture, and initial inventories
3. Down payment (if you are buying an existing restaurant)
4. Closing costs (if you are buying an existing restaurant)
5. Minimum amount of working capital needed to maintain inventories and have enough cash on hand and in the bank to pay bills
6. Deposits for rent, utilities, telephone, sales tax, payroll tax, and furniture and equipment leases
7. Operating licenses and permits
8. Preopening marketing expenses
9. Renovations or remodeling
10. Loan fees (if you are borrowing money)
11. Preopening labor expenses
12. Prepaid insurance expenses
13. Other prepaid expenses, such as consulting, accounting, legal, and security expenses

14. Franchise or exclusive distributorship fees

15. Contingency fees

16. Other miscellaneous expenses

RETURN OF INVESTMENT
Payback of the initial
investment.

RETURN ON INVESTMENT
Payment of some interest in-
come on an investment.

You need to generate enough profit to pay off your loans, pay back your initial investment (**return of investment**), and pay some interest income on your investment (**return on investment**).

Consider the following example. You have a five-year lease at a local shopping mall. You compute that the initial cash outlay must be $100,000. Over five years, you need to recoup the $100,000 plus a return on the investment of, say, about 20 percent. Each year, then, you should generate enough profit to pay back one-fifth of the initial investment ($20,000) plus approximately $15,000 to $20,000 each year in interest income. Your goal in this situation should be to generate approximately $35,000 to $40,000 per year net profit. As with the lease issue, if your gut tells you the location can generate that much money over the five-year period, it might be a good business move for you; at least it is worthy of more thorough analysis.

Some restaurant operators will sacrifice some of this profit for various reasons. For instance, if you have a longer lease, you might be willing to spread the profit out over a longer period of time. If you own the real estate, then you can take less profit during the years and cash out later on when you retire and sell the property. The same is true if you have any other type of reversion asset (such as a valuable liquor license) that can be sold for a nice gain if or when you decide to call it quits.

Some restaurateurs may be willing to forgo a bit of annual profit as a fair price to pay to be their own boss. That's not a good idea. If you are an active owner/operator, you should pay yourself a fair salary and deduct that amount as a normal operating expense when calculating net profit. You do not want to buy yourself a job. Sooner or later, you will get tired of making everyone else rich.

OTHER KNOCKOUT CRITERIA

There are a handful of other criteria that should be considered before you decide to investigate a potential location more thoroughly.

Visibility (Exposure)

In most cases, a restaurateur would prefer having an operation that is easily seen by customers. An added advantage is if persons who don't normally patronize your type of restaurant at least are exposed to it on a regular basis. A lot of people don't drink Coke; however, if they see the Coke sign everywhere, sooner or later they might try it. The same is true for any retail business. If it's continually in a person's line of sight, sooner or later he or she might give it a try.

Zoning

If your business idea violates current zoning ordinances, you must decide whether it's worthwhile to petition for a change in the law. For instance, if you like a particular location, but the law forbids a drive-through window, you must decide whether you want to fight it. If you don't want to fight, or if you think a fight is fruitless, you should eliminate the location.

Utilities

Does the location have the utilities you need? Are the drainage, sewage, power, and so forth, adequate? Not only do you need adequate utilities, you need appropriate ones. For example, you probably would not want an all-electric facility; it would cost more to operate and would not allow for consistent cooking and rapid heat recovery.

Loss of Grandfather Clauses

You might encounter a situation in which an existing restaurant enjoys one or more grandfather clauses. You need to be very certain that they do not expire with a change of ownership. For instance, you don't want to find out after you've purchased the business that you must bring the property up to current building code standards. Since this type of expense is usually very high and very unpredictable, you should walk away from the location if this type of grandfather clause will expire once you take over the location.

Parking

A lot of parking doesn't guarantee a successful operation, but the lack of secure, controlled parking can be devastating. It is very hard to determine how much is enough; local laws usually specify only the bare minimum amount of parking needed, not the ideal amount. You might have to spend time visiting the area during different times of the day to gain a firsthand look at the situation. If you have any doubts about the available parking, it's best to ignore the location.

Lease Term

If the term of the lease would be less than five years, it is not a good idea to accept the location. You need a reasonable amount of time to get your investment back, plus a fair amount of interest income on the investment. Unless it's a very unique case, anything less than five years isn't enough time to accomplish these financial goals.

Property Size

Is the location big enough to house the type of restaurant business you wish to open? Alternately, if space is a little tight, can the interior be inexpensively laid out and designed to overcome operational problems? Size is also a crucial factor if you need to generate a large number of customers to attain your financial goals. It's great to get the smallest property size that fits your needs because the lease payment will be cheaper. But if there is any doubt, it may be better to have a bit more space than not enough. Getting more space today might also be essential if you feel that your restaurant enjoys great growth potential. The additional space will allow you to expand easily; in the long run, it can be cheaper than moving to a new location.

Accessibility

Customers have to be able to find your place and access it conveniently. Unless you have a unique restaurant that people will go out of their way to find, an inaccessible location is almost impossible to operate profitably. If you are located on a very busy street with high traffic speeds, on a major bend in the road, at the top of a hill, or on the wrong side of a street median, customers may not have enough time to slow down and turn in to your parking lot. In fact, according to the father of contemporary restaurant location analysis, John Melaniphy, the two most critical aspects of a location are *visibility* and *accessibility.* If your location comes up short in these two areas, it's best to move on.

Social Barriers

Some people may prefer not to visit a particular neighborhood if, for example, they feel it is unsafe. They may not want to drive up a hill in the winter. Or they may not want to park too far away from a restaurant. Ask yourself whether your typical customer would be willing to visit this area. If the answer is no, or even maybe, it is time to move on to the next location.

Licenses and Permits

You will need at least a general retail business license and some sort of health permit. If you serve beverage alcohol, you will need the appropriate liquor license. You should determine up front whether these are easily available or transferable. You also should ascertain how much the initial cost will be. Don't assume anything when evaluating the licensing needs and the procedures required to obtain them. It is not unusual to see a business that's ready to open experience a licensing delay or denial at the last minute.

TRADING AREA

You cannot calculate accurately your estimated initial investment, annual sales revenues and expenses, and annual net profit without examining the location's trading area. Before you make the final conclusion that the lease expense is affordable and feasible, and that the initial cash outlay is reasonable, you need to verify your estimates with a trading area analysis.

TRADING AREA The neighborhood from which all, or at least the majority, of a restaurant's customers come.

A restaurant's **trading area** is the neighborhood from which all, or at least the majority, of its customers come. It encompasses a radius surrounding the location. For quick-service restaurants located in a downtown corridor, the trading area is usually quite small, perhaps only two or three city blocks. Full-service restaurants usually enjoy a much larger trading area, easily five miles or more.

Restaurants that specialize in the breakfast and lunch business usually serve a small trading area, whereas dinner and lounge operations normally attract customers from a wider area.

According to the NRA, dinner and lounge patrons are typically willing to travel more than twice as far as lunch patrons to get to their favorite restaurants. Travel time, therefore, is a critical consideration. It's especially important if your guests are primarily senior citizens; they overwhelmingly prefer very short travel times.

Unless a restaurant is located in a major traffic-generating location (such as a large shopping mall, airport, or major office complex), its breakfast and lunch customers will travel only about 10 minutes, whereas its dinner and lounge customers will typically spend 30 minutes or more to get there.

You need to draw a trading area around the location that conforms to these travel times. This will give you the most reasonable and most likely area from which the vast majority of your revenue will come.

The trading area will not usually be a circle surrounding your location. Typically, there will be one or more geographical barriers (lakes, rivers, highways, large planned urban developments, stadiums, street endings, and so forth) that make it inconvenient for guest travel. Generally, customers tend to conduct their business and leisure activities on one side of a geographical barrier; hence, the resulting trading area will be a uniquely shaped "blob" on the map.

Once the trading area is determined, you are ready to perform a thorough environmental analysis, the subject of Chapter 3, and a market analysis, discussed in Chapter 4.

THINGS TO DO TODAY

- Eat at a competitor's restaurant.

- Count the number of parking spaces at your favorite restaurant (other than your own).

- Attend a restaurant's going-out-of-business auction, preferably one ordered by a lender or bankruptcy judge. Ask other attendees why they think the place closed. Why do you think it closed?

---

http://tca.unlv.edu/profit

3

ENVIRONMENTAL ANALYSIS: WHAT AM I UP AGAINST?

You do not operate your restaurant in a vacuum. You have to know what's going on around you. You must keep track of what's happening inside and outside your operation, paying attention to things that can impact your business. The best way to do this is to check out your trading area and any other surrounding areas that might affect your restaurant. This can be accomplished by conducting an environmental analysis every once in a while.

We suggest taking at least a little bit of time for this each day. Ideally, you should perform a thorough analysis about every six to nine months. This is an appropriate time frame, in that you do the work often enough to spot important developments, but not so frequently that there isn't enough time for new issues to crop up.

ENVIRONMENTAL ANALYSIS
Environmental scanning, to alert owners and managers to emerging or shifting trends.

Environmental analysis is extremely important. Often called *environmental scanning,* its primary objective is to alert owners and managers to trends that are emerging, shifting, accelerating, or slowing down. Another major goal is to alert decision makers to potentially significant changes before they gel, thereby giving you sufficient lead time to plan for them.

Some operators do not want to spend time gathering this sort of market intelligence. Stay away from this crowd. Don't put yourself in the position of reacting to everything. Once you go down this road, you will constantly be on the defensive. You can't run a successful restaurant if you're always looking in the rearview mirror. You have to look straight ahead, while simultaneously picking up on the warning signs along the way. The more accurately you can predict what will happen, the better chance you will have to surpass your competitors.

The investment needed to acquire this type of information is small, at least in terms of cash outlay. For a minimum amount of money, you can gather and exploit a great deal of valuable intelligence. For instance, analysis of public documents can reveal development plans for new restaurants and products. Interviews with industry analysts and volunteers working with the Small Business Administration (SBA) can yield tips about upstart companies. Internet searches of government documents, articles, speech transcripts, and so forth, can provide indications of pending increased regulations, product shortages, and population trends. Local colleges and schools with food and beverage programs can also be valuable resources, as their faculties and students oftentimes keep up with industry trends and perform valuable research that yields beneficial results.

Although this work is not usually very costly, it can be very time-consuming. But what else is new? If you're going to do well in this business, you'd better get used to spending a good deal of your time paying attention to little details every day. The only way you can coast is to head downhill.

Ideally, if you have a little money and time to spend, you could use the **SWOT Analysis** technique to plan and organize your environmental scanning activities. This technique forces you to divide your work into four key areas that define and/or impact your restaurant: Strengths, Weaknesses, **O**pportunities, and **T**hreats.

> **SWOT ANALYSIS Evaluation of four areas that impact your restaurant: Strengths, Weaknesses, Opportunities, and Threats.**

A restaurant's **strengths** are typically defined by its reputation, location, employees, ambience, view, market share, and so forth. Its **weaknesses** are usually just the re-

> **STRENGTHS Unique advantages you have.**

> **WEAKNESSES Things to avoid or areas that need attention and improvement.**

verse of its strengths. For instance, a good reputation is a strength, whereas a poor reputation is a weakness. Having a lot of parking is a huge advantage, whereas inadequate parking, or inconvenient parking, can be a major weakness.

When assessing your restaurant's strengths and weaknesses, it is important to be honest with yourself. If something is bad, it's best to face up to it. Recognizing that you have a problem is the first step in solving it. Before you sign the rental contract, try to ascertain those weaknesses that you can't control. Don't be overly optimistic, and don't think that once you're open and running you can alter a bad situation. An operator might be tempted by a low monthly rent, which encourages the operator to overlook a critical shortcoming, such as the lack of parking, inconvenient access, insufficient electrical power, or poor layout and design.

The lack of parking is an especially serious weakness. A Las Vegas family restaurant, part of a national chain, occupied the corner pad in a small shopping center. Everything was fine until all the in-line stores leased up and it became apparent that all of the businesses were open at approximately the same times. Ordinarily, you would expect shops in this type of strip shopping center to have varying parking needs—but not this time. The restaurant soon went out of business because patrons could not find convenient parking. Apparently, the operation was not unique enough—did not have that "wow" factor—to overcome this problem.

Opportunities are anything you notice that could potentially have a positive effect on the restaurant industry and, more specifically, on your business. When viewing opportunities, however, you must be sure that they are feasible for your particular operation. For example, there may be a need in the local marketplace for a certain type of menu item. But if you cannot obtain the foods consistently, or if you can't afford to invest in the equipment needed to prepare and serve it properly, you may have to ignore it and consider other possibilities that are more affordable.

> **OPPORTUNITIES   Anything that has a potentially positive effect on the restaurant industry and, more specifically, on your business.**

Threats are any factors that could have a negative effect on the restaurant industry and/or your restaurant that you can do something about. Your analysis will usually indicate something that you need to be concerned about. For example, if your typical customer's average age is mid-thirties, and you notice that more older folks are moving into the neighborhood, eventually you will have to revise your operation in order to attract these new residents. Your response to this type of situation might be to enhance your décor, revamp your menu, and/or adjust your prices. Alternatively, you may decide to sidestep this problem by moving away and focusing on a different type of restaurant operation.

> **THREATS   Anything that has a negative effect on the restaurant industry and/or your restaurant that you can do something about.**

The environment in which you will operate creates opportunities and threats, and you usually have little control over them. They can affect your restaurant and your customers, sometimes unpredictably. It is, therefore, important to make sure you prioritize them. Some may require immediate action, others might wait, while still others may never affect you. Uncovering threats and opportunities is only half the battle.

SWOT Analysis includes past and present environmental changes, evaluating their causes, identifying the critical factors that could be influenced by these changes, and predicting how business conditions could change in the future. The results of this work can guide your planning process. Interpreting future changes can provide clues about things that you should enhance, avoid, or overcome.

You should look at as many aspects of the business world as possible. Be creative. Be willing to consider things that, at first glance, may seem trivial or irrelevant. For instance, restaurant operators should keep up with as many current computer technologies as possible to see if there is something that could be used to increase business efficiency. To that end, owners or managers should read online and print newspapers, magazines, books, and so forth. Creative operators might also want to read materials that their customers read and listen to their customers' favorite music, in order to understand their customers' mind-sets. While the results of some of these activities may have little direct relevance to your operation, they will supply you with the big picture. Thinking in broad terms will enable you to spot future trends a lot more easily.

Successful management of restaurants and other foodservice operations depends to a great extent on the owner's or manager's ability to adapt to a rapidly changing environment. An effective environmental analysis will provide you with specific, timely, and accurate information about societal conditions, competition, the foodservice industry, and government issues that could affect your operation.

TRADING AREA

As a restaurant owner or manager, you should keep up with trends in your local trading area. But, just as important, you need to be aware of broad-based changes on the horizon in our society or culture that could affect the overall restaurant industry. For example, as families "nest" or "cocoon," will take-out and delivery service become more important? Are there legislative trends, such as no-smoking laws, that could impact the bottom line? What about unionization? Keeping up on the big scene is more difficult than scanning your own trading area; however, things that happen at the edges of your radar screen will eventually affect your day-to-day business.

The two most critical trading area components to examine are competition and customers.

Competition

Competition for the eating-and-drinking-out dollar is fierce. Owners and managers who are the last to recognize competitive pressures, and the last to react, are no longer in business or are struggling to survive.

Competitive intelligence can make the difference between being a leader or a follower in your trading area. When used properly, it becomes a tool that can help you protect your market share and possibly increase it.

When analyzing the competition, try to determine the total amount of eating-and-drinking-out dollars currently spent by customers in your trading area. These data are invaluable and will give you an idea of how much money there is to go around, indirectly telling you how hard you have to fight to protect and increase your share of the pie. You might be able to obtain these numbers, or at least a good guess, from your suppliers, the local restaurant association, or sales tax officials.

A time-effective and efficient method of gathering relevant information is to mystery-shop the competition. This is a good way to keep up with what and how other restaurants in your area are doing. For instance, chain restaurant companies usually give an allowance to their unit managers to pay for these visits.

You should consistently know the following about your competitors:

- Number of restaurants in the trading area.

- Diversity of restaurants. For example, what is the ethnic breakdown? Price breakdown? How about the different types or levels of service offered?

- Types of competitors. There are two basic types: the **direct competitor,** who is after the same customer as you, and the **indirect competitor,** who sells food and beverage but is not usually going after the same type of guest.

  > **DIRECT COMPETITOR** A competitor who is after the same customer as you.

  > **INDIRECT COMPETITOR** A competitor who sells food and beverage but is not usually going after the same type of guest as you.

- Entry barriers potential competitors must overcome. For example, to compete in a particular market, an operator may need a liquor license. But how easy or difficult is it to obtain one? If licenses are scarce and you are lucky enough to have one, you may be able to relax just a bit—but not too much! A potential competitor may try an end run by applying for an exemption.

- Who are the especially successful competitors? What can you learn from them and implement in your own establishment? It is a good idea to benchmark the competition. Benchmarking is the process of determining who is the best, say, in terms of service level, value, and food variety. Who sets the standard? What is the standard? If you know, then you can plan strategies that help you reach or surpass that standard. You should determine how the best got to be that way and determine what you need to do in your restaurant to approach that level. If you don't know what the standard is, you can't measure yourself.

- Affiliation of competitors. For instance, if there are a lot of chain operators, they can hold out a long time in a tough, competitive environment. Not so for the typical independent restaurateur.

- Marketing strategies used by your competitors. These strategies focus on the seven Ps of marketing (see Chapter 1). All competitors—including you—manipulate these seven Ps. Some are better at it than others. The best way to tell who the winners are is to look at as many competitors as possible. This will help you immensely; it will give you a good idea of what to do and, more important, what not to do.

- Signature items sold by your competitors. What are their main moneymakers? Can you match them or do them one better? For instance, a lot of operators try to imitate Outback Steakhouse's "Bloomin" Onion. If you try this, make sure that your version is at least as good—and if you want yours to be a big seller, it would have to be a better value.

- Competitors' strengths/weaknesses. As the motivational speakers like to remind us, you should always "dribble to your right." Don't try to go head-to-head with a competitor who is especially skilled in a particular aspect of the business. For instance, you have to be at the top of your game to challenge companies such as P.F. Chang's or The Cheesecake Factory, competitors who know how to hold up well in a murderous, competitive environment. Better to let those opportunities go by. Instead, try to stake out a turf where you can rule, where the other operators will be reluctant to challenge you.

- Are there any market niches vacant? For instance, is there a good reason why no one offers a certain type of menu item? Or is this an opportunity waiting to be exploited?

- Competitor life cycles. Do operations open and close all the time, or is the area stable? Either way, you want to be on the right side of the cycle. For instance, an unstable competitive environment usually means there is no compelling reason for guests to visit the local restaurants. If so, you have to do something to stand out, something that compels customers to visit you over and over. If possible, try to focus on one or two competitors' life cycles. How did they start? How did they handle their preopening? What significant changes did they make along the way? If they went out of business, was it because of operational problems or uncontrollable things, such as a major rent increase?

Customers

Every restaurant seeks to serve a specific target market, or market segment. This market should be defined clearly, preferably before you select the location.

You can develop your restaurant concept, theme, menu, and so on, then go around looking for a location that has the target market you believe to be the best match. Or you can find the location first and tailor your restaurant to the target market that resides in that trading area. Using the first approach, you are typically more satisfied with the results, since you would be working in an establishment that you like. In the second case, you might be able to develop a successful operation, but if it isn't exactly the type of restaurant you feel like owning or managing, you may eventually become negative about it. On the other hand, when using the first approach, finding the proper location for your specific needs might be difficult or too expensive, whereas in the second scenario, there might be more opportunity to produce favorable results. Oh well, if this stuff were easy, anyone could do it.

If there are several target markets in a trading area, it is vital that you determine which ones best match the strengths of your restaurant. This is critical because, as they say, you can't be all things to all people. Furthermore, if a particular market segment is not a good match for your type of food and service, it is fruitless and expensive to develop a marketing strategy that attempts to attract those guests. It is much better to select the one or two segments that match up well with your property. In this way, your marketing strategy is more likely to yield positive results.

It is a good idea to at least consider more than one potential market segment and whether the potential customers in those segments would be satisfied with the type of food and service you will be offering. You don't want to unnecessarily and unknowingly ignore a target market that may be somewhat marginal today but could grow into a significant profit contributor with a little bit of attention. For example, you may not want the hassle of take-out business in your full-service restaurant. You should consider it, though, if you are located near state government offices, colleges, or an industrial complex. Guests who have been introduced to your restaurant through a take-out experience may become regular in-house diners someday.

Similarly, a full-service restaurant operator may want to open for lunch and dinner instead of dinner only. These days, it can be very difficult for a full-service operation to make money at lunch. However, people who lunch at your place may come back for dinner sometime and bring their friends or families with them. Or those who work on your side of town but live at a distance may be good lunch customers, but they would probably not make the trek back for dinner. If you can attract enough of these folks, it can be financially rewarding to stay open during this part of the day.

Ultimately, you usually have to home in on one main segment and adjust your resources and marketing strategy accordingly. While it may be appropriate for you to service more than one segment, sooner or later a unique segment will make the most sense for your restaurant.

Things you should consistently know about the customers in your target market include the following.

Demographics

Demographics are the statistical characteristics of human populations in specific geographic areas. Things such as number of people, ages, gender, income levels, and employment are related to the eating-out and drinking-out behavior of consumers. For example, a lot of two-income households in the trading area would indicate the potential for considerable dinner take-out business. A large retiree population usually indicates a good deal of early-bird

> **DEMOGRAPHICS The statistical characteristics of human populations in specific geographic areas, such as age, income, education, type of employment, and type of household (such as single, married with children, married without children).**

dining business. Baby boomers typically reflect a market segment that dines out a lot and is interested in trying new foods and beverages.

Demographic information can be found in census reports and on Web sites (see, for example www.censusscope.org). These data are also available from private companies that sell current statistics tailored to your needs (such as www.thirdwaveresearch.com).

Psychographics

Psychographics are consumer characteristics that are based on people's lifestyles. They include things such as their personalities, where they live, habits, leisure activities, ideologies, values, beliefs, and attitudes. Attitudes are especially useful

> **PSYCHOGRAPHICS Consumer characteristics that are based on lifestyles.**

bits of information for any retailer, and they include things such as propensity to save, work ethic, acceptance of alternative lifestyles and cultures, willingness to accept risk, brand loyalty, and adaptation to cutting-edge technology.

Psychographics give us better insights into marketing behavior than demographics, but they are very difficult to measure. Most people do not like telling strangers about their personal lives. But these days, we don't have to ask them. Providing information about people is a big business. Market research firms know which of your customers go on cruises, have children under five, live in town-houses, are single, and so on. Heck, these companies even know what you had for breakfast today and where you parked your car last night. They base their work on things such as people's credit card history. Using this information, a company like Gazelle Systems can categorize restaurant customers based on lifestyles. For one restaurant, Gazelle was able to describe its customers as interested in a healthy lifestyle, consumers of fine wines, international travelers, and likely to try new things on the menu. This is certainly more useful than telling you that your average customer is married, age 45, and female.

Shifts in Your Current Customer Base

You need to have a good idea of your current customer profile. Who are your customers? Where do they come from? Why do they like to visit your operation? How much do they like to spend? What types of service do they demand? If you don't know these kinds of things, you won't be able to tell if your customer base is changing. Sooner or later, most customer bases will shift. You need to anticipate this and be prepared. Demographics and psychographics can provide useful insights and indicate future trends. Working the dining room and getting to know your guests can yield equally valuable information. (Since you can never know too much about your guests—and about potential guests—we have devoted all of Chapter 4 to this important subject.)

OTHER THINGS TO CONSIDER

You should try to keep up on the latest political, legal, technological, and economic developments that occur in our society. It is important to think globally, because the world is now truly a small place. Political realities in another part of the world can easily influence us at home.

In the political and legal arenas, you should be alert to potential legislation that could significantly impact your operation. For instance, what would happen to you if the federal government decided to eliminate the tax deduction for employee meals? What about a ban on harvesting sea bass? Or an increase in the minimum wage? Closer to home, what would be the impact on your bottom line if the local city council decided to change the zoning laws to allow more taverns to open in your trading area?

Technology does not always strike us as being that critical in a service business. But few restaurants can afford to ignore it. For instance, how will the declining cost of inventory-tracking software impact your day-to-day operating expenses? How will virtual reality options affect restaurants that offer a video game entertainment? These things change very quickly, and innovators in this area generally fare better.

The local, national, and international economies can be excellent harbingers of eating-and-drinking-out sales revenue potential. A little slip in gross domestic product (GDP), a downturn in the stock market, a bump in interest rates, or a slight increase in the unemployment rate can kill some restaurants. On the other hand, such developments can actually benefit other restaurants. For instance, after the tragedy of September 11, fine-dining establishments took a bath. Customers couldn't afford the high prices they charge. How-ever, since these customers still wanted to eat out, they merely traded down to lower-priced restaurant operations. Hence, neighborhood restaurants with casual themes experienced sales increases.

Fortunately, this type of information is consistently tracked, interpreted, and reported by the National Restaurant Association (www.restaurant.org). Cost of membership is very small compared to the amount of valuable assistance the association can provide. As a bonus, if you belong to the national group, usually you automatically become a member of your state restaurant association.

Other information that can be critical in the restaurant industry is the type and amount of labor available that you can tap for your operation. Having an appropriately sized staff with the necessary skills to do the job is essential, as it will influence what you can prepare and serve to your guests. In addition, you should find out as much as possible about the cost of labor in your area. Prevailing wage rates and employee benefits must be tracked and estimated very carefully, especially before you decide to open a new restaurant or make a significant change in an existing property. Local and state labor departments and unemployment offices usually can supply such data; if not, they can point you in the right direction.

THINGS TO DO TODAY

- Order an updated census report for your trading area from www.censusscope.org.

- Find out what magazines your customers read and subscribe to some of them. Encourage your employees to read them now and again and brief you about trends they think might affect your business.

- Check out the number of new building permits issued in your trading area last month.

---

http://tca.unlv.edu/profit

4

IDENTIFYING MARKETS: WHO ARE MY CUSTOMERS AND WHAT DO THEY WANT?

Being able to identify your target markets (i.e., market segments), implies two things: one, that you have gathered the information needed to understand the differences between market segments, and, two, that you know which market segments are patronizing your restaurant.

To create value for your customers, you must understand who they are and what they want. Understanding what appeals to your customers will help you create the competitive advantage you need to succeed.

Understanding the types of people you attract and why you are attracting them may also uncover information about complementary market segments that you've never considered. It may turn out that these segments are worth pursuing after all.

MARKETING INFORMATION

In Chapter 3, we discussed how to keep up with external changes so you can react to them appropriately. In this chapter, we'll talk about how to gain specific information about the people who walk through your doors every day. Armed with this information, you can more easily give them the best possible value and experience.

A good example of how to gather and use this type of information was noted in a recent issue of the *Cornell Hotel and Restaurant Administration Quarterly.* John F. Power, general manager of the New York Hilton and Towers, used Japanese market data to develop a breakfast menu that would attract this market segment and encourage repeat patronage. Based on the information gathered, Power stated, "I realized how different a Japanese breakfast is from our own." He also observed, "While most people like to sample the cuisine of the country they are visiting, everyone prefers to eat familiar food for breakfast." As a result of these insights, the New York Hilton now serves miso soup, nori (dried seaweed), yakizanaka (grilled fish), raw eggs, natto (fermented beans), oshiako (pickled vegetables), and rice as part of an authentic Japanese breakfast buffet. This strategy gave the New York Hilton a competitive advantage over other hotels vying for this target market.

Gathering market information can be very expensive, but it isn't really necessary to spend a lot of money on this task. Anybody can pay thousands of dollars to a marketing research firm. Forget that. It's not practical for the typical restaurant operator. Let's discuss some techniques you can use yourself to gather meaningful marketing information about your customers.

Employees

The most overlooked source of information about your customers is your staff of employees. Employees can describe the customers who create the most value for your restaurant. They know who the big spenders are. They know the ones who are not price sensitive, those who come back on a regular basis, and those who tell their friends about your place. Employees can describe who these customers are, so you can group them into segments. These employees can also tell you what the customers like, so you can serve them better.

One of the most useful data-gathering techniques to come along in our industry in recent years is the **listening posts** concept. You should think of your service employees as microphones placed around the room. Employees listen to what guests are saying about your operation and your competitors.

> **LISTENING POSTS** The practice of having your employees listen to what guests are saying about your operation and about competing operations.

They should be trained to write down guest comments on a pad in the service station and turn them in at the end of the shift.

Managers should categorize these comments and look for trends. Some trends will be favorable, but some may highlight things that need your attention. For example, counter workers in a casual service restaurant may overhear customers complain that they have to pay for soft-drink refills. Your guest-service staff might hear about a new restaurant in your trading area that your customers love or complaints about the service at a competing restaurant.

Your customers are talking about you and your competitors. You can improve your profitability by capturing this information. If customers are complaining about being charged for soft-drink refills, you might discuss this issue with some of them to see how widespread this feeling is and what they think about possible options. For example, you might ask them what their reaction would be if you provided refills, but only after you increased the drink prices, say, to $1.75 from $1.25.

If some of your guests are chatting up a popular new restaurant, it should prompt you and your staff to visit this place and determine what your response to the new competitor should be. On the other hand, if a competitor's service is dropping off, this should prompt you to communicate (i.e., promote) your own excellent customer service to your target markets.

In order to set up a good listening post system, your employees have to trust you. Before they will relay information, they need assurance that you will use it in a positive manner. For example, if a food server remarks that customers are complaining of overcooked steaks and the next day there is a new broiler cook, the employee may feel that this information caused the cook to get fired. Actions like this will shut down the information sharing in a hurry. Alternatively, if the server comes in the next day and sees the cook getting some additional training, then it becomes apparent that these comments had a positive influence and led to a favorable result. Moral of this story: Management actions taken as a result of the comments received through the listening post system need to be as positive as possible, plus they need to be communicated to the employees so they can see how their efforts enhance the entire operation.

When you go out to another restaurant, you tend to look around and see what those folks are doing that might work in your operation. You don't go out to eat so much as you go out to taste and to spy. Well, guess what? Your employees do the same thing. Sometimes managers forget that their employees view themselves as being in the restaurant business. They are critically evaluating other restaurants the same way you do.

Many managers fail to debrief their employees. In addition to telling you about the customers, employees can also give you information about concepts and practices they've seen at other restaurants that could work at your restaurant. You should have occasional meetings with your staff—say, every month—to collect this type of information. The starting point for finding out who your customers are and what they want is your employees.

Record Keeping and Purveyors

In addition to employees, your record-keeping system and your purveyors are great sources of customer information. Sales trends can be especially useful. For example, a manager noticed that sales of a chicken breast entrée, topped with sautéed mushrooms, were slowly declining. Up until the point at which sales began to fall off, this item had been one of the restaurant's most popular dishes. This manager was concerned about this, so she started asking customers about the dish. She quickly found out that the pool of butter on the bottom of the plate, which once had been viewed as a delicious mushroom-butter sauce, was currently viewed merely as grease. She immediately revised the dish to broiled chicken with a side garnish of mushrooms that were well drained. Sales rebounded nicely.

Internal records can also let you know how your customers are reacting to price increases. For example, if you decide to bump up several menu prices after performing a menu engineering analysis (see Chapter 5) and you begin to notice fewer appetizer and dessert sales, or if you see that less expensive entrées are increasing in popularity, it may indicate price resistance. If there is an increase in menu prices but no increase in the average check, this can also validate your market's unwillingness to increase its spending.

Suppliers are excellent sources of information. While you may not always have time to stop and chat with every purveyor, it usually pays to stay in touch with them. They tend to be the gatekeepers of information and gossip floating around in your trading area. For instance, they can keep you abreast of new food trends, potential product shortages, what's popular with restaurant patrons these days, who's going broke, who's looking for a job, potential product price increases, and so forth. Your suppliers are part of your operation. Their relationship to you is similar to the one you have with your other employees. Sure, they show up primarily to sell you something. But they are also there to help. Take advantage of their expertise.

Customers

You need to collect information about your customers, so that you understand what they value most when selecting a restaurant to visit. This knowledge will help you create a competitive advantage.

CUSTOMER ADVISORY BOARDS
Groups of customers who meet with you regularly to provide feedback on your operation and competing operations.

A growing trend in the restaurant industry is the use of **customer advisory boards.** These are groups of customers who meet with you regularly—say, monthly or quarterly. The meeting is typically structured around a group meal or reception.

An advisory board is a good way of getting customer feedback about things such as changes you're thinking about making in the restaurant, how customers like changes you have made in the past, and things other restaurants are doing that might work for you. For example, if you are thinking about changing the menu, starting a new promotional campaign, or remodeling the facility, run it past your advisory board. Their feedback is usually very candid and to the point.

This brings up an interesting issue: can you sit there quietly and listen to people criticizing your operation? You have to have a thick skin if you set up an advisory board. The members want to do the right thing and are not afraid to tell you if they think you're on the wrong track. Furthermore, their suggestions may not always be feasible, or implementation may be impossible for one reason or another. You risk alienating your board if you ignore their advice too often.

GROUP INTERVIEWS Usually a group of three to five customers who are asked to respond to a set of questions posed by an interviewer. Elaborate dialog is usually part of the process.

If you don't have the time, or the stomach, to cultivate an advisory board, consider conducting periodic **group interviews.** These usually consist of different individuals selected randomly from your repeat clientele. Group interviews can be just as valuable as advisory boards. They may even be a shade better since you can rotate participants more easily. You can also meet only when it's necessary; there is less pressure to stick to a structured schedule.

In a recent issue of the *Cornell Hotel and Restaurant Administration Quarterly,* Joe Welch tells about a steak house suffering from declining sales. The owners set up group interviews with two sets of customers in order to get a handle on this problem. One group was composed of customers who indicated they would return, and the other group was composed of those who said they would not. During the group sessions, the owners learned that patrons considered the restaurant a fun place, but thought the food was boring. Expanding and revising the menu solved the problem.

A story in *Restaurants USA* illustrates the power of group interviews and the kind of information customers can give you that you might never think of yourself. Andy Reis of Café Provincial in Evanston, Illinois, found that his clientele wanted valet parking. Since there was on-street parking as well as a nearby parking garage, Reis always assumed that parking was not a problem. He also found that his diners felt uncomfortable in the restaurant's Terrace Room, a casual dining room with glass tables and porch furniture. Andy loved it, but apparently it was too casual for his diners. Based on this feedback, he remodeled the room and added valet parking. Now people request to sit in the Terrace Room. Reis states that having a dialogue with groups of customers is worthwhile if you listen carefully to their input.

Exit surveys can be a good way of gathering useful information from your customers. For example, customers can be asked to rate different attributes of your restaurant, such as food, service, menu variety, value, and overall restaurant experience. A 1-to-5 rating scale is often used, whereby 1 = poor, 3 = average, and 5 = excellent.

EXIT SURVEYS Customers can be asked to rate different attributes of your restaurant upon leaving the establishment.

If some folks rate an attribute 1, 2, or 5, ask them to write down why they gave the attribute an excellent or below-average rating. Knowing you got a 2 on food does not give you much information, but knowing you got a 2 on food because the customer ordered a baked potato and it did not come out until the guest was almost done with the rest of the meal gives you a specific detail that indicates what you need to do to correct the problem. In fact, in this example, it may indicate that what the customer perceived as a food problem was really a service problem. Thus, you often need to collect more than just numerical ratings before taking action.

Another type of analysis we like to make is comparing ratings of the attributes listed in the survey to respondents' behavioral intentions, such as their willingness to return and to recommend the restaurant to others. The numerical ratings of individual attributes can be used as benchmarks. For example, let's say you got a 3.75 overall rating on service, but those who said they definitely intend to return rated service 4.35. This means that you need to improve your overall service rating to 4.35 to create more repeat business. This could be a great discussion topic at your next customer advisory board meeting or group interview session: how can you improve your service?

CUSTOMER SATISFACTION SURVEYS Similar to exit interviews, but they may be done at any time, not just at the end of a meal. For instance, they might be conducted through the mail or on the Web.

After conducting several **customer satisfaction surveys** of this type, you will find that respondents who give you a 5 on the overall dining experience are the repeat patrons. Typical survey results will also show that 80 percent of those who rate you a 5 (excellent) will say they definitely intend to return. However, this percentage declines by half (to 40 percent from 80 percent) for those who give you a 4 rating. Usually only 40 percent of those who rate you a 4 state that they definitely intend to return. The irony of this phenomenon is that many owners and managers feel good about getting overall ratings of 4.2 or 4.3, because this is between good and excellent. But the fact is that there are many good restaurants. It is the excellent ones, the ones with that sharp competitive edge, that catch the continuing attention of your target markets.

If you decide to do surveys, it is not a good idea to have your staff collect the information. Customers will recognize them and may not give candid responses. An inexpensive alternative to using your own staff is to ask the marketing class at a nearby university or community college to do the surveys as a class project.

Another good data-gathering technique is also one of the easiest: talking with customers every day. Talking with guests can be a great source of information if you let them know you want their honest feedback.

Greet customers in the dining room and ask them specific questions about your operation. For example, if you see them eating a new menu item, ask them what they think about it. Most people will tell you it is all right since they do not want to say anything negative. Therefore, you need to tailor your questions to address concerns you might have about the product, for example: Is the sauce sweet enough? Was the meat as tender as you expected? Is the portion size adequate?

You should also ask other probing questions: Is the service and food as good as the last time you were here? Is the noise level acceptable? Is there anything we can do to improve?

If you are thinking of adding new menu items, take a sample plate out to your regular customers to see what they think. When you notice new customers, introduce yourself and welcome them to the restaurant. Ask them how they found out about you.

You can also test promotional deals on your customers. For example, a supplier may offer you a promotional special on wine if you buy ten cases. But instead of buying ten cases, buy one case and sell each bottle at the price you would charge if you took advantage of the promotion. If your customers think it's a good buy at that price, then go back and buy the ten cases, or more if you can.

In a recent issue of *Restaurants & Institutions,* Allison Perlick noted how the manager of Zemi in Miami used customer feedback from her upscale market to help create a successful lunch business. She found out that lunch guests wanted a more casual atmosphere and that $20 was the most they would pay—even those lunch customers who gladly paid twice as much for dinner. To attract more of them to lunch, she developed a $16 to $19 menu and installed attractive wooden tabletops that allowed her to remove the table linen at lunchtime. These changes improved lunch sales considerably.

Cinnabon's customers told the company they wanted a place to sit down and enjoy their rolls. Cinnabon responded by developing a redesigned facility that includes customer seating. In locations where sufficient space is unavailable for seating, Cinnabon tries to work with landlords to secure access to common-area seating.

TIPS FOR GATHERING USEFUL CUSTOMER INFORMATION

- Ask your employees to describe your customers and tell you what they like and dislike.

- Use your employees as listening posts.

- Debrief your employees on concepts they have seen in other restaurants that could be implemented in your operation.

- Sift through your records to identify trends.

- Use a customer advisory board or group interviews.

- Make a point of talking to customers every day.

- Use customer exit surveys or other types of customer satisfaction surveys to identify what you are doing right and what needs to be improved.

MARKET SEGMENTATION

Market segmentation is a process of determining who your customers will be. To attract profitable customers, you must understand the target markets (i.e., segments) available to you and select the ones that will be interested in your products and services. The end result of

MARKET SEGMENTATION A process of analyzing your trading area to determine who your customers will be.

market segmentation is the development of a set of one or more target markets that are a good match for your restaurant.

The market segmentation process involves three steps: segmentation, targeting, and positioning.

Segmentation

The first step in this process is to identify all potential segments that might be interested in your type of operation. The segments available will vary by type of business. For example, families are a viable market segment for fast-food and casual restaurants, but they are less viable for upscale restaurants. The type of restaurant you operate determines the type of market segments that you will be able to attract.

There are many ways to segment restaurant customers. The most common are as follows:

- *Demographics (see Chapter 3).* Typical **demographic** variables used in **segmenting** restaurant markets are age, income, education, type of employment, and type of household (e.g., single, married no kids, married with kids).

  > **SEGMENTING** Identifying all potential market segments that might be interested in your type of operation.

- *Behavioral.* **Behavioral segmentation** divides markets according to how and why they use restaurants. For example, Pizza Hut became the number one pizza

  > **BEHAVIORAL SEGMENTATION** Divides markets according to how and why they use restaurants.

  restaurant chain in the United States by developing a nationwide chain of sit-down restaurants. But Domino's knew there was a market segment that preferred eating pizza at home. This option was particularly appealing to families with young kids, since they didn't have to hustle getting the kids ready to go out and worry about how they would behave at a sit-down restaurant. Since no one would dine in its restaurants, Domino's would need smaller and less expensive sites than Pizza Hut. Little Caesars noticed yet another opportunity: pickup. The company became famous for giving customers two pizzas for the price of one, as a reward for picking them up. By using market segmentation procedures successfully, Domino's and Little Caesars were able to enter a market dominated by Pizza Hut.

Other behavioral characteristics include benefits customers seek from a restaurant and the type of occasion motivating a guest to visit a restaurant. For example, some people go to a restaurant to celebrate a birthday, while others go simply because it is lunchtime and they are hungry.

Sometimes you can influence a target market's behavior. You may be able to shape it just a bit. For instance, Amy Spector noted in *Nation's Restaurant News,* that Bob Evans Farms developed a "carry home kitchen" concept to encourage carryout after the senior vice president of marketing discovered that 50 percent of all meal occasions in the Bob Evans Farms trading areas were off-premise or carryout. By streamlining the take-out process, Bob Evans was able to create additional value. Customers responded by purchasing more take-out meals, resulting in a nice bottom-line increase for the company.

GEOGRAPHIC SEGMENTATION Divides the market into geographic units.

- *Geographic.* **Geographic segmentation** divides the market into geographic units. These may range from a few blocks for a downtown restaurant to entire countries for a multinational chain.

- *Psychographics (see Chapter 3).* **Psychographic segmentation** divides the market according to lifestyles. For example, some people will go to exclusive restaurants because they want to be seen

> **PSYCHOGRAPHIC SEGMENTATION** Divides the market according to lifestyles.

and confirm to others that they have an elite lifestyle. Some people want to go to a neighborhood sports bar because they enjoy socializing with people who share common interests, such as loyalty to a certain sports team. How people live and how they perceive themselves influence how they select retail operations to patronize. In most cases, the restaurants people choose reflect who they are—or, at least, who they think they are.

Targeting

Understanding how a market can be segmented will help you identify the best ones to target, as well as those you should avoid. For example, if you have a casual restaurant that attracts young couples, say 25- to 40-year-olds, you should not accidentally develop a marketing program that might bring in families. When people go out to eat and drink, they prefer being with people like themselves. Childless couples like to go to a restaurant where they will find similar couples. Families want to be with other families. This reassures them that they are in the right place.

Instead of targeting a different market, a casual restaurant should look for related segments that will complement the existing market. If, for instance, it does not have a Sunday brunch, a champagne brunch may appeal to the existing market in addition to drawing other guests who wouldn't patronize the restaurant at other times. For example, the House of Blues at the Mandalay Bay in Las Vegas has a Sunday Gospel Brunch that draws some customers who do not represent this club's typical guest the rest of the week.

Effective target marketing requires you to find market segments that complement your existing market or markets. Juice bars originally focused on baby boomers who wanted healthy fast food. Eventually some of the juice bar chains discovered there was a segment of college students equally interested in healthy foods. Result: These chains have successfully expanded onto college campuses. They serve the parents and grandparents at home and the children at school.

With a little thought and creativity, many other types of restaurants may be able to employ this sort of target marketing. Sweet Tomatoes, a family restaurant, is a case in point. It features a salad bar, pasta bar, fresh baked goods, and excellent soups. Its wholesome food also appeals to both seniors and singles.

Many restaurants serving several market segments have even successfully targeted the school market. For example, elementary schools often have limited kitchen facilities. There may be an opportunity in your area to serve your food at a school once a week, or you may be able to cater special events hosted by the school.

Panera Bread restaurants serve cold, deli-style sandwiches on fresh bread, along with hot soups. This combination attracted more women than men. A story in *Nation's Restaurant News* describes how the company developed a selection of panini sandwiches as part of its effort to attract more men to its restaurants. Offering hot sandwiches proved effective. They brought in more men and helped increase store sales by over 5 percent.

A story published in *American Demographics* provides another good example of how a restaurant company identified a complementary market segment and then developed products that would attract it. Bill Watson, vice president of marketing for Steak and Ale Restaurants, found that empty nesters (older couples without children living at home) represented less than 20 percent of Steak and Ale's customer count, but generated a much greater share of sales revenue. His research verified an NRA study concluding that empty nesters spend 65 percent more on dining out than do couples with children at home. As a result of this research, Steak and Ale developed new menu offerings to satisfy the baby boomers who are fast becoming empty nesters. One of these products is a "nine-pepper filet." This product piques the taste buds of diners in their fifties. Older folks generally like these types of menu items because, as people get older, flavors create different sensations. Restaurant operators should experiment with unusual flavor combinations in order to attract this market segment.

Sometimes, you have to make several changes in your day-to-day operating procedures if you decide to go after a new market segment. For example, some restaurants, especially those located near assisted living centers that provide shuttle service to their residents, have decided to target the growing senior citizen market. These restaurants should know that seniors like price discounts, such as early-bird specials. They prefer smaller portions, low noise levels, large-print type on the menus, and bright, secure restaurants. They also are slower diners than most other segments. This means that restaurants targeting seniors must train their servers not to rush; the service desired by a business customer will give seniors the impression you are trying to rush them out the door.

Positioning

Positioning is perception; it is the image of your restaurant that you want to firmly embed in your customers' psyches. Whenever your restaurant's name pops up, you want customers to immediately understand who and what you are.

> **POSITIONING** The image of your restaurant that you want to firmly embed in your customers' psyches.

Restaurants need to position themselves in such a way that they are not viewed as a commodity, but as something different, something unique. Ideally, there would be no confusion; your image must be clear and concise.

Ultimately your customers determine your position. For example, McDonald's image is a place for families with young children, whereas Wendy's is seen as a place for adults and families with older children. However, you can take actions to help position your restaurant in the customer's mind.

Whenever a restaurant wants to position, or reposition, itself, it may need to make several changes and adjustments. This might involve something as simple as pointing out the obvious. For example, initially, no one perceived Subway as a health food restaurant. Nevertheless, many of the company's products are healthful alternatives to other fast-food choices. So Subway now runs a series of ads stating that several of its sandwiches are low in fat and calories. It even hands out discount coupons at local health clubs and gyms. Subway has successfully repositioned itself as a healthy alternative to fast-food meals.

Burger King's "Have It Your Way" campaign is a classic example of a restaurant managing its position. The company ran these ads when McDonald's operating procedure was to have a buffer inventory of sandwiches waiting under the heat lamp. At McDonald's, you placed your order, and the server took the prepared sandwiches from the rack and put them in a bag. It was a great system for speed, so long as the guest didn't want a special order. If, say, someone wanted a hamburger with extra pickles and mustard, he or she was given a special order slip and had to wait. Burger King realized this was a negative for many customers, so it developed the "Have It Your Way" campaign to differentiate itself from a major competitor.

Pizzeria Uno is another good example of repositioning. Pizzeria Uno started out as an adult pizza place, positioning the restaurant as distinct from Pizza Hut and other family pizza restaurants. As it evolved, it began expanding its menu to attract couples to the restaurant more frequently. According to a recent article in *Restaurant Business,* pizza currently accounts for only 18 percent of the restaurant's sales revenue. To capitalize on this trend and to reposition itself as a casual restaurant, Pizzeria Uno changed its name to include "Chicago Bar & Grill."

In a recent article in *Restaurant Hospitality*, Katie Smith described how Friendly's repositioned itself from an ice cream stand catering primarily to children to a casual restaurant. Scott Colwell, Friendly's vice president of marketing, said the company was well known for sandwiches and ice cream, but not as a place where families should go for dinner. He wanted to reposition the restaurant as a place where guests would come for lunch as well as dinner.

Colwell believed that parents were pressed for time and often felt guilty about not spending more time with their children. If he could create a dining experience that both children and parents would enjoy, the family would have fun together.

To find out what would make a good dining experience for children and parents, Colwell conducted focus groups with children. One of the issues that came out of the focus groups was that children wanted "real" menus, like those given to their parents. They didn't want place-mat menus. The kids also told the interviewers what kind of food they wanted and how they wanted it presented. Friendly's decided to put a kids' coordinator on each shift to ensure that the children's needs were met and that the parents were comfortable with everything.

According to image research done before and after the program, Friendly's effort to reposition itself as a family restaurant was successful. Recognition of this new image—that Friendly's was a good place for kids and their families—jumped 50 percent.

Notice how Friendly's used marketing research to find out about the market it wanted to target. The marketing information it gathered helped the restaurant chain to understand the family market and its unique consumer behavior. Knowing that kids play a major role in restaurant selection, Friendly's created a program to make it a place children would want to go to and bring their parents.

THE HEART OF THE RESTAURANT CUSTOMER

What kind of generalizations can we make about the typical restaurant customer? *Is* there a typical restaurant customer? Professor Valerie Zeithaml has done extensive research into this issue. She contends that restaurant patrons exhibit a few common characteristics.

1. When thinking about going to a restaurant for the first time, customers rely primarily on information from personal sources. They will ask the opinions of friends, relatives, and acquaintances they consider knowledgeable and trustworthy. If they must rely on strangers, they will seek out people who they think are familiar with the restaurant business, such as a hotel's front-desk employees or its concierge.

    Restaurants should attempt to affect positively those persons potential customers may contact. For example, in larger cities, there is a concierge association. Smart operators seek to host this club, thereby letting the members experience their restaurants so that they can give accurate advice to hotel guests.

2. Customers determine that a restaurant was great *after* they have experienced the food and service. Restaurants provide experiences that are difficult to judge beforehand. All of your first-time customers are taking a chance; they are there on a trial basis. If you give them excellent product and service, if you meet or exceed their expectations, odds are they will come back and tell their friends. If you don't make the grade, they won't return; they'll also tell their friends about the disappointing experience.

3. Customers often use price as an indication of quality. A person who enjoys fresh seafood and sees grilled red snap-

per on the menu for $7.99 may assume that it is a low-quality, frozen product since fresh domestic red snapper is usually priced twice as high. When using price to influence demand, care must be taken to ensure that you don't create inaccurate consumer perceptions about product quality. If you're not careful, you could accidentally give the impression that your place is cheaper or more expensive than it really is.

4. Before customers purchase restaurant meals, they usually feel that they are taking some risk. They can't "test-drive" the product ahead of time. So it's only natural that they are somewhat apprehensive, at least until they get to know you. You need to be sensitive to this feeling because so many people today eat out in a group, with friends, acquaintances, business contacts, clients, and so forth. If your customers want to impress their associates, they will almost always take them to a favored restaurant they have visited often. If your establishment is one of these operations, you'll enjoy this type of loyalty—the best loyalty of all. Not only do you get the return patron, but you get his or her associates. Talk about leveraging your sales revenue!

5. Customers often blame themselves when they are dissatisfied. For example, a person who orders seafood gumbo for the first time at a new restaurant may be disappointed with the dish but not complain because he blames himself for the bad choice. He loves the way his favorite restaurant fixes seafood gumbo and thinks he should have known that the new restaurant would be unable to prepare it the same way. When the food server asks how everything is, he replies, "Okay."

    Employees must be aware that dissatisfied customers may not complain. They should be alert to potential sources of guest dissatisfaction so they can address them quickly. In this case, the food server should notice that the guest is not eating the gumbo and should indicate that the restaurant would be happy to replace the dish with an alternative dish that could be prepared and brought out very quickly. This can turn a negative into a positive—and, usually, it doesn't cost you anything because most of the time the guest will decline an alternative. However, you will make points with the guest, who will appreciate the gesture.

THE MIND OF THE RESTAURANT CUSTOMER

How does the typical guest make a purchase decision? Is a purchase at a restaurant primarily an impulsive decision, or is it planned? Probably somewhere in between. One thing's for sure, though: your customers undergo a series of stages when they make the purchase decision. Understanding these stages can help you develop a marketing approach that will attract your target markets.

Triggering the Purchase Decision

There has to be an event that triggers the purchase decision. This could be as simple as hunger pangs telling a person it's time to eat. It could be that the customer is programmed to eat out at noon. It could also be a special occasion, such as a birthday. Perhaps the person had a stressful day at work and decided to go out rather than cook at home.

It is important to understand the events that trigger your customers' purchase decisions. Think of it like this: the guests have a problem, you are the problem solver. For example, McDonald's, knowing that many of its customers visit because they do not want to cook at home (problem), developed its "You Deserve a Break" (solution) advertising campaign.

Special-occasion restaurants try to obtain the birthday and anniversary dates of their customers so they can send them a congratulatory note and a small gift coupon redeemable at the restaurant, for such items as an appetizer, a glass of wine, or a dessert. During the holidays in December, many organizations have parties. Those restaurants with banquet rooms will send out notices at the end of September or early October, reminding organizations that they can cater their events.

If you understand what motivates customers' purchase decisions, you can show them how your restaurant can solve their problem. You can answer their question: "Where should I go today?"

Information Search

The second stage is the information search. Sometimes, customers go through an extensive search; other times, they have a set of restaurants they consider. For example, a person deciding to go out to a casual restaurant to take a break from eating at home may have four casual restaurants from which to choose. If your restaurant is not among the **choice set,** you need to do something to break into it or else your restaurant won't be considered. This can be accomplished with a promotion that catches the customer's attention and gives her a reason to come to your restaurant rather than one of the restaurants in her choice set.

> **CHOICE SET　A short list of restaurants that customers consider when deciding where to go when it's time to eat.**

If the meal is for a special occasion or the guest is on vacation, the search will be more extensive. Guests on vacation typically spend a great deal of time planning their meals. If they aren't eating, they're thinking about eating. In such cases, it is important to understand the information sources that guests use. If they are on vacation, do they ask the concierge at the hotel? If they are looking for a specialty restaurant, do they check restaurant guides, local newspapers, the Yellow Pages, the Internet? If you know where your target markets

TIP OF THE CENTURY

Understanding your customers is the core of a successful marketing program. You need to know who your customers are, what they want, and how they make their purchase decisions. Without this information, you cannot market effectively.

search for information, you can make sure the name of your restaurant comes up when the guest is searching.

Evaluation of Alternatives

The next stage is the evaluation of alternatives. Customers will zero in on one of the alternatives in their choice set. If you are in that set to begin with, then you have a fair chance of being their eventual selection. Recall the Pizzeria Uno example earlier in this chapter. The company knew that when its name popped up, guests would see it as merely another pizza restaurant. Thus, if the restaurant customers did not want pizza, the company's restaurants were immediately dropped from the choice set. This is why the company repositioned itself; it wanted to remain in the choice set, even if pizza was not the desired meal.

Restaurant customers will usually evaluate the alternatives based on attributes they consider important. If your restaurant rates higher than the competition on key attributes, you will have a greater chance of getting their business and getting it more often. This is why you need to survey guests now and then; it is critical to know and understand what is important to guests when they select restaurants.

Selection Stage

The final stage is the selection stage. This is when the determination is made by the customer or group of customers who want to dine out together. Up until this stage, your restaurant is one of several in a choice set. To be chosen, you will need to make a final push and influence the person or persons making the ultimate decision.

It is important for you to know who the decision makers are. You can get a good idea of who these folks are by talking with your customers regularly. You can also uncover this type of information from the NRA, which publishes several reports every year detailing this and other, similar types of insights.

Knowing who influences the purchase decision will help you develop effective promotions that target them. For example, children play an important role in the choice of a fast-food restaurant. This is why fast-food restaurants advertise to them.

Research also shows that when determining where a family will eat, kids have a major influence. In fact, children influenced over $110 billion in restaurant spending in 2001. On average, families with children account for 56 percent of all dollars spent on food away from home.

Besides the kids, it is also useful to consider their parents' concerns. For example, at a recent Kids' Marketing Conference, parents told restaurant managers that comfortable seating was important because their kids squirm in hard seats. They also said they did not like play areas in sit-down restaurants; they wanted to be with their kids all the time. They also expect more nutritious meals in a sit-down restaurant than they do in a fast-food restaurant. Furthermore, parents mentioned that it is important to have servers who can deal with children.

THINGS TO DO TODAY

- Go to www.restaurant.org and check out the research reports produced by the NRA.

- Organize a focus group of a few of your guest-service staff employees.

- Ask the next customer you see what prompted him or her to visit your operation.

5

MENU DEVELOPMENT: WHAT SHOULD MY SALES KIT LOOK LIKE?

A menu is much more than a list of the restaurant's offerings. It is a valuable marketing opportunity, a blueprint for profit. It is your opportunity to show what your restaurant can offer. The items listed, as well as their presentation on the menu, will draw the attention of every guest who enters your property.

One of the nice things about the restaurant business—one of its main advantages over other types of retail establishments—is the fact that almost every guest who comes through your doors, or contacts your take-out or delivery service, wants to buy something. They're not just shopping around as they do in other retail establishments. In fact, it's estimated that, at most, only about 50 percent of visitors to the typical retail operation will buy something.

Your guests are in the mood to spend money. And usually they are happy when they arrive. Given all these pluses, it is up to you to make sure these positive vibrations continue. Since the menu is the one thing that every guest will see and it immediately creates one of the restaurant's first impressions, it is one of the most critical parts of your operation. A positive first impression will help keep the guests happy and keep them coming back.

The menu is your single most important advertisement: it is your primary means of communicating with guests. It must be of the highest quality possible, consistent with the image you are trying to create and sustain. A high-quality menu will include the correct items, prices, descriptions, and appearance. It will also be clean and tidy, up-to-date, and mistake-free. Furthermore, it must be clearly understood by the service staff so that they can answer questions and make appropriate recommendations.

A high-quality menu can entice customers and generate sales. It can have a tremendous influence on how much a customer will spend. It is an integral part of any successful marketing strategy and must convey a stimulating message that will be received favorably by your target market.

WHAT TYPES OF PRODUCTS SHOULD I PUT ON THE MENU?

You can develop a list of items that you especially want to produce and serve to your guests. If this is your preferred strategy, make your menu selections first; then you will need to hunt for an appropriate restaurant location. You must design and open your restaurant in a trading area that is consistent with the kinds of menu items you plan to offer.

Alternatively, you can find a location that you can afford and is available, and then work up a menu that will appeal to the guests in that particular trading area. This strategy may not be as appealing, but it does offer more options and more opportunities than the first.

Regardless of how you address these concerns, there are a few critical things that must be considered when deciding upon the types of items to include on the menu. What you can offer on your menu depends on the resources you have. The resources with the most influence on your menu planning options include the following:

- *Layout and design of the facilities.* Unless you're willing to spend a great deal of money, an existing location may restrict your menu offerings. For example, you would be hard-pressed to offer outdoor dining if the necessary plumbing and energy hookups are unavailable. You can accommodate these needs if you are building a restaurant from scratch. Unfortunately, while the initial menu of a new restaurant may make sense with the layout and design you have, future menus may not enjoy this advantage. Probably the best thing to do is to find locations that offer a great deal of flexibility.

- *Availability of food and beverage ingredients.* A consistent supply is not assured. For instance, if you wish to offer certain types of wines to your guests, you will need a dependable and adequate allocation from your distributors; otherwise, you will be frustrated when your repeat customers ask to be served their favorite beverages and you find you have none in stock. A related factor is seasonality. If you include seasonal ingredients on your menu year-round, you will have to pay a premium for them during the off-season.

- *Type of equipment.* If you have a lounge or tavern operation, the equipment, as well as the layout and design of the facilities, will usually accommodate several types of beverage menus. This is not the case with food menus, though. The more elaborate the food menu becomes, the more equipment you'll need. You'll also need more sophisticated, expensive equipment. Ideally, you should have flexible equipment that can be adapted to several needs.

- *Labor.* As noted briefly at the end of Chapter 3, the amount and skill level of the available labor pool will have a significant impact on what you can prepare and serve. You must have enough employees with the appropriate skills in order to produce the required volume. Say, for example, you want to upgrade your menu by including more fresh-foods preparation, but this is not currently possible with the labor you have. You may be able to fudge just a bit by purchasing upgraded food production equipment to accomplish the same result. Or you might purchase ingredients that have undergone some limited prepreparation, such as precut meats. In the long run, though, such solutions can be too expensive and might also eliminate that human touch that diners prefer.

- *Budget.* You must consider the amount of money the average guest is willing to spend in your type of operation. If, for example, your customer base is economy minded, your menu items must play to this mind-set. Don't offer overly expensive menu items that are inconsistent with this type of market.

- *Customer desires and needs.* Your customer base usually changes and evolves little by little. One day your guests can't get enough fat, sugar, and salt. The next day they want their french fries cooked in canola oil. You need to stay on top of your target market so that you can plan for and respond to your guests' ever-changing tastes.

WHAT TYPES OF MENUS SHOULD I USE?

There are many possible ways of presenting your menu items to guests. You should try to determine those that offer the best merchandising and profit potential. Typical kinds of menus to consider include the following:

- *Meal part (day part) menus.* These are menus that focus on a particular meal. For example, you might consider a separate menu for each day part: breakfast, lunch, dinner, high tea, snack, and so forth.

- *Cycle menus.* These are menus that repeat themselves according to a predetermined pattern. For instance, you might decide to offer a specific list of specials each day, so that, say, every Wednesday you serve pasta specials, every Thursday you serve salad specials, and so on. Cycle menus can be very important if your target market is a captive audience. For example, if your restaurant is located next to a college campus, you may want to offer some items on a rotating basis so that the students won't become bored with your restaurant.

- *Drink lists.* In some cases, it can be a good idea to have a separate wine list, drink list, waters list, and so on. These have great merchandising appeal, and they can free up space on the food menus, making them more attractive and easier for guests to handle. They also offer servers the opportunity to interact with guests, thereby giving them the opportunity to upsell and increase the average check.

- *Dessert menus.* These menus also offer great upselling opportunities. They work even better when, instead of a printed menu, you have a dessert cart or tray that you can use to showcase the products.

- **Daily menus.** Given the ease and efficiency of desktop publishing, you could conceivably print a different menu each day. More likely, you could print one that contains mostly the same items every day, but also includes highlighted specials—similar to the way many fresh seafood houses merchandise their daily catches or wine bars merchandise the wines of the day or week.

- **À la carte menus.** These menus list a price for every item, so that the guest pays a separate price for each dish ordered. There are no "combo" meals or "value" meals.

- **Fixed-price menus.** These are sometimes referred to as "bundled," "prix fixe," "all-inclusive," or "table d'hôte" menus. They are the opposite of à la carte menus. There is one price for a set meal or a set combination of items.

- **Downtime menus.** These are usually limited menus, with lower prices, offered during normally slow periods of the day. They are intended to boost sales revenue during these times. Examples are the early-bird special menus, late-night menus, and midmorning break menus offered by restaurants that are open 12 to 14 hours a day.

- **Casual menus.** These are sometimes referred to as "limited" menus. They are similar to the downtime menus; however, they are not priced as low, and they typically offer a little bigger selection. A limited menu is useful if you have a small kitchen, but a large dining room and lounge, where speed is essential. Having fewer menu items doesn't place as much stress on the back of the house, which allows you to turn the tables quickly.

- **Café menus.** These are menus used by high-end restaurants that wish to offer patrons a choice between the regular (higher-priced) offerings in the main dining room and a more limited (lower-priced) selection in a separate area of the restaurant. These are similar to the type of menu offered in a country club grillroom, as compared to its offerings in the formal dining room. The idea is to broaden your market, gain more exposure for your operation, and perhaps convert some café customers to main dining room customers down the road. Smith & Wollensky and Spago's are good examples of this concept.

■ *Interactive menus.* Some operations allow guests to mix and match their orders. For instance, Macaroni Grill allows guests to create their own pasta dishes. The guest does this by checking off different options on a card and then handing the card to the food server.

You also see this with "bingo" menus used by some caterers. The caterer has several lists of food and beverage items, each of which is individually priced. The client picks, say, number 2 from column A, number 17 from column B, and so forth. Eventually, he or she ends up with a personalized menu for the event.

This concept also works for the beverage menu. An emerging trend finds the operator inserting the wine list into a computer program that then allows the guest to pair the food order with the wine order. When a guest at the Aureole restaurant in Las Vegas asks for the wine list, the sommelier brings a laptop computer to the table, plugs it in, and shows the guest how to use it. The guest can sort wines by color, price, dryness, and so on. The guest can also ask the program to recommend appropriate wine and food pairings. Guests love it. So does the manager, who can make wine menu revisions instantaneously. Furthermore, printing and related costs are eliminated. One drawback: Guests tend to play around a lot with the technology, thereby slowing table turns a bit. Consequently, this option may not be feasible unless you run a high-priced operation.

- **Tabletop displays.** These can be used effectively to promote your moneymakers, but only if you minimize the amount of copy. Customers don't usually read them. You have to let pictures tell the story if you use table tents to supplement your menus.

- **Catering menus.** Those restaurants that offer catering, either off-premise or on-premise, usually have some sort of separate catering menu. Some do not want to use a separate menu, preferring to build each party from scratch—that is, they develop a custom menu for guests who would like to incorporate their personal preferences into the menu. If you have printed catering menus, however, keep in mind that customers may review them in their homes or offices, where you will not be present to guide their choices and sell the event. By the time you meet with these customers, their initial choices may have been made. The menu itself, and any other related materials you hand out, must convince these customers to have the event at your property. These materials must contain enough information to sell the event without you around. To do this, make sure that you highlight any awards, testimonials, favorable reviews, chef's credentials, and the like. By the way, don't forget to plug your catering department on your other restaurant menus and any supplemental promotional materials.

MENU LAYOUT

You should avoid a cluttered look when designing your menu. There should be roughly 50 percent blank space on any type of menu or menu board, so that it does not appear crowded. In addition to the

blank space, it should have wide margins and sufficient space between menu items. A crowded menu is difficult to read, which could
turn off some guests. A crowded menu design also makes it difficult
to highlight the moneymakers you want to promote.

Course headings serve to divide the menu into various categories, such as appetizers, salads, entrées, and desserts. These headings should be in a larger and/or bolder type than the rest of the
menu.

A category should fit on one page. It should not carry over to
the next page or overlap another category. Guests will usually review
a category only down to the bottom of the page or to the next course
heading if the category is less than a page long.

Menu items should stand out. They should be bigger than the
descriptive wording that accompanies them, but smaller than the
course headings. If you use descriptive wording (food ingredients,
preparation method, etc.) for each menu item, be certain that it is
clear and to the point. Avoid rambling descriptions; let the servers fill
in any additional comments should the guests ask for more information about a selection.

Menus should be centered symmetrically for aesthetic appeal.
Symmetry is pleasing to the eye and tends to allow for enough blank
space to be attractive, as opposed to filling the page with print and
illustrations.

Be sure to include in a prominent position on your menu the
name of the restaurant, address, phone number, e-mail address, Web
site address, and any other pertinent location information.

If you put up a menu board, you must be very succinct. You
must keep it up-to-date and maintain it properly. Missing letters,
outdated photographs, or taped-over prices will make people think
twice about patronizing your establishment.

With menu boards, you must capture the guests' attention
quickly. Most customers will not read the entire board until after
they place their order. You need to use as much visual stimulation as

you can afford to direct their attention. The Cadillac of menu boards is the digital, moving display. Any movement is better than no movement. However, this might be too costly for the typical restaurant operator.

It might prove worthwhile to create a unique menu layout that will make the guests feel they are patrons of a trend-setting operation. For example, instead of organizing a wine list according to countries or colors, consider organizing them according to whether they are sweet or dry. Another possibility is to categorize them as "New World" and "Old World" wines.

MENU COPY

It is important to write copy that helps create and maintain your restaurant's image in the customer's mind. Descriptions of menu items should generate interest and sales. The copy must speak to guests in their own language. Be concise in your verbiage, but make your points. Get your message out as efficiently as possible.

The copy should convey mouth-watering images, using phrases such as "delivered hot and fresh," "crisp," "succulent," or "flaky," depending on the dish you are describing. The language used should not be bland. For instance, instead of listing "Assorted Cheeses," say: "An Array of Creamy Brie, Tangy Muenster, and Sharp Cheddar Cheeses."

Avoid clichés, such as "the best-kept secret," "chef's special," and "as you like it." Also avoid words such as "rich," "heavy," and "thick," which unnecessarily worry weight- and health-conscious customers. Furthermore, make sure you use words that actually describe the menu item; what is a "surprise omelet"?

The *Cornell Hotel and Restaurant Administration Quarterly* published an interesting study, performed by researchers at the University of Illinois at Urbana-Champaign, who discovered that menu descriptions evoking favorable feelings can boost restaurant sales by approximately 27 percent. Furthermore, study participants considered these menu items to be of higher quality and value compared to the perceptions of persons who consumed the same items without benefit of the descriptive wording.

Be consistent in your writing style. Avoid mixing casual phrases with dignified statements, which tends to confuse guests.

Well-written copy can assist guests in making the proper choices. It can also steer them toward ordering your most profitable menu items. It can prevent confusion about dishes, and it will be especially helpful to guests who may not devote too much time to reading the menu because they are involved in conversation with others at the table.

If your menu doesn't include copy that touts your on-premise catering offerings, party platters, take-out options, and so on, you are missing a great opportunity to make additional sales and profits. You might consider printing separate menus for these products and services, ones that can be given to inquiring guests. If you do this, you must be absolutely certain that the menus are accurate and thorough, because guests usually put more deliberation into catering decisions. Decisions of this type are often made by more than one person, whereas decisions made on the spot at the restaurant tend to be much more impulsive.

The copy should not overestimate the customer's knowledge. You may need to explain menu items, ingredients, preparation methods, and the like, which may not be readily understood or easily recalled. For instance, younger folks today may not know what Veal Oscar is. A similar situation can arise if you use foreign terms. For instance, if you list "Kartoffel Kloesse," you should include the descriptor "Savory Potato Croquettes."

It is a matter of opinion whether you should include menu copy that describes the operation, its history, and so forth. Although it may not do anything to drive sales and profits, it can help create an identity for the restaurant. The big problem with this type of copy, however, occurs when it is not revised regularly. If you write it up today, it will be current and contemporary, consistent with today's vocabulary. But a year from now, it could sound severely outdated, and you might fail to recognize that.

When preparing copy, pay attention to these guidelines:

- Do not capitalize prepositions ("with," "in," "or," "of," "between," "under," "over," "from," "around," "along," etc.). Prepositions in French ("au," "aux," "du," "en," etc.) also are not capitalized.

- Do not capitalize articles or conjunctions ("the," "a," "an," "and," "but," etc.).

- Depending on the context, capitalization of verbs such as "served" or "filled" is optional, so long as you are consistent. When a verb is used as an adjective in the name of a dish (e.g., "Stuffed Mushrooms"), it is always capitalized.

- Be sure to use correct spellings: "potato," not "potatoe"; "béarnaise sauce," not "bernaise sauce"; "Hashed Brown Potatoes," not "Hash Brown Potatoes"; "iced tea," not "ice tea"; "Brussels Sprouts," not "Brussel Sprouts."

- Discard any menu if it contains typos or grammatical errors. You should never use correction fluid or try to write over such errors. You will have to dump the menus and order new, correct ones.

- "Filet" is for meat; "fillet" is for fish.

- Do not use "w/" for "with," or "&" for "and." Avoid abbreviations.

- When referring to potatoes, rice, or pasta, do not use the word "starch." Starch is for shirts.

- "Scalloped Potatoes" and "Escalloped Potatoes" are both correct. "Pimiento" and "pimento" are both correct.

"Welch Rarebit" and "Welsh Rabbit" are both correct. Just be consistent.

- "Barbeque," "barbecue," and "BBQ" are all correct. These are regional differences in spelling. "BBQ" is more casual, but this is generally a casual menu item.

- "Crawfish" and "crayfish" are both correct. They are regional differences. However, it is always pronounced "crawfish."

- "Catchup," "catsup," and "ketchup" are brand names. Check the container for the right spelling.

- Manhattan clam chowder is made with tomatoes; it is red. New England clam chowder is made with milk or cream; it is white.

- The correct spelling is "hors d' oeuvres." When used in a title, capitalize the *H* and the *O,* but not the *d.* Canapés are a type of hors d'oeuvres, with a bread or cracker base.

- Avoid using the word "entrée" for the main course. Refer to it as the "main course." In some parts of the world, the word "entrée" refers to the appetizer.

- Do not list prices from least to most expensive. This looks like a laundry list and may subconsciously make customers shop for price instead of for specific menu items.

ILLUSTRATIONS/GRAPHICS

Menus should incorporate at least some graphics and illustrations, which add a great deal of visual appeal and can stretch the customer's imagination. They are also very effective in highlighting your most profitable menu items. While you may be able to minimize their use on a typical restaurant menu, it is a good idea to include several of them on catering menus.

You can find all sorts of free, high-quality clip art on many Web sites. Or you can purchase inexpensive CDs or special software programs that contain a wide variety of art that you can use on your menu.

The ultimate graphical element is the professionally done photograph, but this can be the most expensive option. Photographs of activities are more effective than photographs of inert objects, such as a photograph of your facilities, and they work especially well on catering menus. Prospective catering clients can project themselves into the setting depicted in the photo, which might persuade them to choose your facility for their events.

If you plan to use food in the photographs, it's best to use close-ups of finished products, rather than just the raw ingredients.

Avoid overdone, common photos, such as a shot of a smiling chef standing next to a buffet table or working in an open kitchen. Strive for a fresh approach. Be unique. There is no point in spending a great deal of money for generic photographs that will be ignored by customers.

Bad photographs are worse than no photographs. The best quality and most expensive is the four-color (full-color) photo. When you are looking at a four-color photo, you are actually seeing an assemblage of colored dots. The dots are thicker where the colors are darker. The color separation done during the printing process determines the final quality of the photograph.

MENU TYPEFACE/FONT

There are hundreds of different typeface styles and sizes from which to choose. Use those that make the menu as easy to read as possible.

Times New Roman is the standard font used on Windows-based PCs and is part of the Times family of fonts. There are extended families, such as Goudy, Century, Swiss, Gill, and Garamond.

Use extended font families because they work well together—not only for menus, but for other things you may want to print, such as nameplates, place cards, and party announcements. Thus, we recommend that you stay with the same family, using the following variations:

Plain lowercase

PLAIN CAPITALS

Bold lowercase

BOLD CAPITALS

Italic lowercase

ITALIC CAPITALS

Bold italic lowercase

BOLD ITALIC CAPITALS

Do not use a font smaller than 12 point. If your target market is senior citizens, you should use a larger size.

Avoid the Courier font, which looks like the old-fashioned typewriter font. It does not have a modern, professional appearance.

Fonts can be used to draw attention to your most profitable menu items. For instance, you might consider using a unique font to highlight menu specials. Or you might use an unusual font to describe the nonfood products you sell, such as logo merchandise and other kinds of souvenirs.

Menus must be user-friendly and easy to read. For example, ALL CAPITALS CAN BE DIFFICULT TO READ. Menus that are difficult to read can irritate customers. Catering menus that are difficult to read may just be scanned quickly and discarded.

Desktop publishing can give you the flexibility needed to incorporate several fonts. It also gives you the ability to change menus quickly, easily, and inexpensively. Although desktop publishing is a useful process, it should be done by someone who has sufficient knowledge to do it attractively and professionally. It's not the kind of thing that can be learned by reading a few instructions. Consider purchasing software to simplify the process. You can find such software through www.ranw.com/MENUPRO/menupro/main.htm. Don't compromise quality and appearance just to save a few dollars.

MENU COVERS

Many menus are printed separately and intended to be inserted into a reusable cover. The two-panel 9-inch by 12-inch cover is a popular format. It is convenient for guests to handle, and it will easily accommodate the standard 8½-inch by 11-inch stationery. This size will also fit snugly into a standard business mailing envelope, which is a plus for catering menus.

If you veer too far from this standard-size bifold menu cover, you will have to pay more. On the other hand, a unique size and/or shape can be a highly recognizable signature that can enhance customer awareness and drive sales revenue.

PAPER STOCK

Be sure to use a good-quality paper stock, consistent with the type of restaurant you have and the image you want to project. With professionally printed materials, about 40 percent of the cost is for paper. The two basic choices are cartridge paper, which has a matte finish, or coated paper, which has a shiny finish. The one you choose is typically influenced by the initial cost as well as the appearance of the color you've selected on each type of paper. The paper's shelf life may also factor into your decision. For instance, coated paper is very attractive, but it tends to crack when folded.

The heavier the paper, the better the impression you will make. Parchment, for example, has a lush texture and conveys elegance.

However, while you may want your menus to have a classical look, you may unintentionally signal to guests that your operation is overly expensive because you are spending too much money on fancy menus. There is a fine line between elegance and wastefulness. On the other hand, don't use paper that is too cheap. For instance, computer paper would be unacceptable for most restaurants. Even something like coated paper could be inappropriate because, unless a professional printer handles it, it does not absorb ink well.

MENU COLORS

Color adds variety and interest to the menu. It can be used to highlight course headings as well as your operation's most profitable menu items. But production costs escalate as you add colors, so it is usually preferable to stick with two colors: the paper color and one ink color. Dark ink on white or light-colored paper makes the best contrast and is easiest to read.

If you are printing menus that will be faxed, dark ink on white paper is the best choice. You want to make sure that the recipient of your fax will be able to read it easily. For instance, if you use gray paper or gray-colored printing, the fax will be difficult to read. Check with the printer to make sure you have an appropriate combination. As a test, fax one to yourself before ordering a big printing job.

Before ordering a printing job, be sure you see a sample of your preferred color on the paper stock you select because the type of ink you choose will look different on different types of paper. If you provide the printer with a sample of the color you want, he or she can determine the best type of ink to use with your preferred paper stock.

As with the paper stock, you should select colors that reflect the type of restaurant you operate. For instance, for a fine-dining establishment, select classic colors for the menu covers, such as deep royal purples, rich dusky blues, dark greens, and chocolate to mahogany browns. These shades are elegant and convey reliability and a sense of permanence. Insipid colors, such as lime green or hot pink, create a faddish appearance. For the paper, a rich cream color will impart a more cultured look than a stark white finish.

Be sure that the print color jumps off the page. It is impossible for a color-blind customer to read red print on a dark background. Likewise, older guests may have special vision problems. Take this into consideration when choosing your color scheme.

TRUTH IN MENU

Make sure that the copy and illustrations or graphics you put on your menu do not violate truth-in-menu laws. It is a violation of the law to mislead customers by misrepresenting what you serve.

In its 1977 report, *Accuracy in Menus,* the NRA noted 11 categories of menu misrepresentations that must be avoided:

- *Quantity.* Portion sizes must be accurate. For instance, if your menu states that your omelets are made with jumbo-size eggs, you must use that product. ("Jumbo" is one of six federal government sizes used in the fresh egg trade.) The biggest problem with quantity is the misleading terminology that sometimes creeps onto the menu. If you offer a "large" bowl of soup, a "supersize" soda, and "mile-high" chocolate cake on your menu, you might consider adding descriptors that note their actual servable weights.

- *Quality.* You cannot advertise a level of quality that you don't provide. For instance, you can't say that you serve crab when you actually serve the imitation "krab." The federal government has established quality grades for many of the foods and beverages we use. Be careful that you don't mistakenly list one of these grades on your menu. For instance, you can't use the word "Prime" to describe your beef offerings unless you are actually purchasing and serving this quality-grade of meat.

- **Price.** Make sure you disclose all relevant charges. If, for example, there is an extra charge for all white-meat chicken or for beverage refills, this should be clearly identified on your menu.

- **Brand name.** Like quality, you cannot imply that you serve a brand-name product if, in fact, you are using a substitute item. For instance, you can't substitute Pepsi if the guest asks for Coke. The problem with brand names is that many of them are not so obvious. We regularly use the term "RyKrisp" to refer to crackers, though, in fact, RyKrisp is a brand name. Likewise with the name "Jell-O." Many of us casually use this term to refer to any type of gelatin product; however, Jell-O is a brand name and can be used only if you serve that product.

- **Product identification.** The federal government has established several "standards of identity." These standards define what a food product must be in order to be called by its standard name. For instance, orange juice is not the same as orange-flavored drink, maple syrup differs from maple-flavored syrup, and pure vanilla extract is not the same as vanilla flavoring. It is easy for many of us in the restaurant trade to slip up and use these terms interchangeably.

- **Point of origin.** This is yet another area where we tend to toss around terms without giving them a second thought. For instance, "Australian" lobster sounds appealing, but if you don't purchase and serve lobster that comes from this part of the world, you cannot use this descriptor. Likewise with descriptors such as "Idaho" potatoes, "Lake Superior" whitefish, and "Iowa" corn-fed meats.

■ *Merchandising terms.* Sometimes you can get into trouble if you use too much trade puffery to describe menu items. You can't, for example, note that a menu item is "made from scratch" if, in fact, some canned ingredients have been used. Nor can you state that you serve "center-cut" pork chops unless you can back up that claim.

■ *Preservation.* Be very careful when using the term "fresh." This term implies that the food ingredients you use have never been frozen, canned, bottled, or dried. You might be able to get away with saying a menu item is "freshly prepared" or "prepared to order," but it's advisable not to push this issue. There will be days when you just can't get a fresh ingredient and have to settle for a frozen one. There will also be times when you have to prepare items ahead of time, even though you prefer preparing them to order.

■ *Means of preparation.* Many guests may select a particular menu item primarily because of the way it's prepared. For instance, health-conscious guests may prefer broiled chicken to fried chicken.

■ *Illustrations/graphics.* Restaurateurs love to place photos of finished food products on the menu, and especially like to show these on menu boards. When you do this, though, you have to make sure that the products you serve look similar to their pictorial representations.

■ *Nutrition.* Since mid-1994, restaurants in the United States have been required to verify any health, nutrition, or dietary claims made on menus and in other forms of advertising. You must also follow appropriate guidelines when using standardized terminology. For example, if you wish to use the descriptor "light" or "lite," the food servings they describe must have at least one-third fewer calories or at least 50 percent less fat per serving.

MENU MANAGEMENT

Of the many factors influencing customer visits to your restaurant, the menu is one of the most important. All of the considerations discussed in this chapter have an impact on the menu's ability to merchandise your business. They should coalesce in such a way that your menu maximizes revenue and profit.

Menu management, sometimes referred to as **menu merchandising,** is a never-ending activity. Seldom does a day go by that you are not either making some

> **MENU MERCHANDISING**
> **Managing your menu for profit.**

menu change or thinking about making a change. Managing the menu should always be uppermost in your mind.

The most effective way to manage your menu is to perform a menu sales analysis, that is, **menu engineering** analysis, regularly. We recommend that you do a menu engineering analysis at least one month after opening

> **MENU ENGINEERING**
> **Evaluating the menu to determine its profitability.**

your restaurant, and at least once every three months thereafter. Armed with data from this analysis, you then should tweak the menu in such a way that future menus will generate more profit.

Get your hands on a sales analysis software package; the point-of-sale computer system you're using may have this software included or may be able to accommodate another vendor's program. If you want to save money, you can create your own software package using the Microsoft Excel spreadsheet program.

The type of analysis we prefer, and the one we teach to our students, is the menu engineering analysis developed by Don Smith and Michael Kasavana when they were both at Michigan State University. The companion Web site to this book offers a homemade menu engineering program, using Excel spreadsheet software, on which you can practice.

The analysis requires you to input the number of each menu item served during the period of time under consideration, the individual cost for each menu item, and each menu item's selling price. The software does all the work after that. Be forewarned though: you must have accurate cost information or the results of the analysis will lead you to erroneous conclusions. No matter how much restaurant experience you have, if you fudge a little when calculating your costs, you may get unreliable results. You have to know your numbers in this business.

STAR   Very popular menu item that is profitable.

PLOWHORSE   Very popular menu item that is not very profitable.

PUZZLE   A menu item that is not very popular, but is profitable.

DOG   A menu item that is not popular nor is it profitable.

The analysis evaluates how popular and how profitable each menu item is and sorts each item into one of four classifications: **Star** (very popular, very profitable), **Plowhorse** (very popular, not so profitable), **Puzzle** (not so popular, very profitable), and **Dog** (not so popular, not so profitable).

A menu item is very popular if its menu mix percentage, or popularity index, is higher than average. The item is very profitable if its gross profit, or contribution margin (CM), is higher than average. Once you know the amount of total gross profit your current menu generates, you should make whatever menu revisions you think will increase that number.

There are many things you can do to effect a profitable menu revision. For instance, let's say you own a restaurant that offers sandwiches, but also offers appetizers and entrées. Many of your guests are ordering the lower-profit sandwiches. You want more of them to order the higher-profit appetizers and entrées. What to do? One option is to relocate the sandwich listings on your menu. Remove them from the center of the page, and perhaps even put them on the back page. Put the appetizers and entrées in the high-profile center space. More patrons are likely to order them if they are highlighted this way.

And don't worry about those sandwiches. The guests who really want them will find them, but the guest who hasn't made a decision yet is more likely to order a higher-profit item.

You might accomplish a similar result by changing slightly the way you list the items on your menu. For instance, try putting the highest-profit menu item in a category at the beginning of the list, and the second-highest-profit menu item at the end of the list. Since the eye naturally travels to these two extremes, guests who have not made a decision before entering your restaurant may be more apt to order these menu items.

While there are all sorts of other things that can be done to squeeze a little more profit out of a menu, the one that usually has the most impact is your menu pricing structure. For instance, you might be able to increase the price of every menu item by 5 cents merely by rounding up every menu price to a whole dollar amount. Over a one-year period, you could potentially pick up a few thousand dollars doing this, and the typical guest is unlikely to recognize what you've done. After all, how much difference is there between $19.95 and $20? Gas stations have been playing this game forever, tacking on nine-tenths of a cent to each gallon purchased. One downside to this strategy is that you can only do it once.

If you have a Star menu item, you may be able to get away with increasing the price a little, but it's a dance with the devil whenever you increase a price. In this case, you need to determine whether the menu item is a Star simply because it's priced appropriately; if you believe this is true, then you might want to leave it alone and look to adjust the prices of other items. Though you can't get too crazy and bump up a Star's price too much (or too frequently), a small bump (say, a dollar) should be acceptable to your guests.

Use the same logic with Plowhorses. Since these dishes are very popular, there's a good chance that you can get a little more money for them from each guest (say a half-dollar). But do make sure that the low price isn't the only reason for the popularity of these items; if that's the case, any little increase may cause a drastic falloff in orders.

Puzzle items might be priced too high, or perhaps the uniqueness of these dishes does not appeal to the majority of your guests. Try dropping the prices just a bit to see if that generates more interest.

Since it's unlikely that you can raise the price of Dogs, they should usually be eliminated. The only valid reasons to keep a Dog on the menu are if it is the favorite of some of your steady customers or if you already have the ingredients in inventory and don't have to purchase additional stock.

If you change your menu offerings, descriptions, positions, prices, and so on, after an analysis, you should allow a few weeks to give the new menu a fair trial run. Don't make further changes too hastily; customers may become nervous if you do that.

However, if you sense, after the first week of a new menu, that one of the items is a Dog, for example, you need to make a change. You don't necessarily have to yank it off the menu immediately, but you can play with the portion size and its presentation on the plate, train the servers to push it, and take other steps to increase the item's popularity. If the item continues to be a poor seller, it should be removed the next time you print a new menu.

Menu merchandising and menu management are a never-ending exercise. You can't simply print a menu and forget it until the next time you do a sales analysis—by that time, you might have missed some great opportunities or, worse yet, allowed mistakes to linger too long. Check out some of the links from this book's Web site (such as www.menusforprofit.com) that highlight the latest trends in menus and menu designs, as well as great menu development and menu merchandising tips.

THINGS TO DO TODAY

- Attend a restaurant trade show and check out the award-winning menus.

- Scan your menu for any possible truth-in-menu violations.

- Gather sales and cost data for a few menu items, and do a practice menu engineering analysis.

---

http://tca.unlv.edu/profit

6

PRICING: WHAT SHOULD I CHARGE FOR THIS STUFF?

The best price is the one that guests are willing to pay and that gives you the profit you need. It's almost impossible to determine what that ideal price is, though. Every guest has a slightly different perception of value. Pricing formulas can't take every variable into account, and, given the fluctuation in the costs of food, beverage, and other supplies you must deal with daily, there is no way you can continually adjust your prices to meet new conditions.

Pricing involves a little bit of science with a whole lot of art. It is unfortunate that such a key part of the marketing plan has to be so inexact, but there is just no one right way to price your products and services.

One thing is certain about pricing: it is very easy to charge too little, leaving yourself vulnerable to bankruptcy. If you look at the major reasons that businesses fail, inadequate pricing is usually high on the list. This is especially true for small, independent restaurants that do not have the large accounting and marketing staff support enjoyed by the major firms.

PRICE VERSUS VALUE

Before considering prices for individual menu items, catering events, or other merchandise, try to determine how much your typical customer is most likely to spend when visiting your restaurant. In other words, what is the most likely average check you can expect to obtain, given the type of business you have and the customers you serve. You can gather this information by reviewing past sales records, or, if you are opening a new business, you can get a good idea of this dollar amount after performing the environmental analysis discussed in Chapter 3.

Let's say you determine that the average lunch check is $10; that is, you anticipate that each guest will spend $10 per lunch visit. If that's the case, you need to decide on the best way to get that $10. For instance, if you develop and price entrées at about $9.95, your typical guest would be unlikely to order anything else, such as a beverage, appetizer, or dessert. But if you price entrées at $6.95 to $7.95, the guest will more than likely order a beverage, a dessert (perhaps one for the whole table to share), or some other item. Guests will perceive that they are getting a greater value if several products can be purchased with that $10 rather than only one. As in other areas of your business, the process of developing prices requires that you think like your typical guest.

Some operators prefer à la carte pricing; others prefer a bundling approach. Fine-dining operations and cafeterias usually price everything à la carte, whereas quick-service, family-style, and casual-dining restaurants typically offer some sort of bundling.

Generally, businesses with lower average checks and more value-conscious customers should offer guests some bundling opportunities.

In a fine-dining restaurant, guests are accustomed to paying individually for every little thing they order, even for such items as bread and water. Cafeteria guests are also used to this type of pricing structure. À la carte pricing works well in these situations. In quick-service places, however, offerings such as "value meals" are very important; guests expect them. Quick-service, family-style, and casual-dining restaurants typically offer a combination of à la carte and bundling pricing methods. They also may have a few all-you-can eat (or "all-the-soft-drinks-you-can-hold-down") specials.

They say that value is in the eye of the beholder. You need to get a firm handle on your guests' value perceptions (see Chapter 1), but it certainly isn't an easy task. Even though you might have a grip on it today, it can easily change tomorrow; you need to focus on this issue constantly.

Value encompasses all of the seven Ps of marketing (see Chapter 1). But it is related primarily to quality, price, and service. There is a direct relationship between quality and price; guests expect higher quality to be accompanied by a higher price. The same relationship exists between service and price; more service and better service cost more. The trick is to find out how far guests are willing to go. What appeals to them? How much will they pay for added benefits? What are their priorities? The list of questions is endless.

Sooner or later, you will develop a feel for what your guests want. It is then up to you to monitor their needs and modify your pricing strategy accordingly.

PRICING FOR THE RESTAURANT MENU

There are a lot of books, articles, workshops, and seminars devoted to menu pricing procedures. It is a topic that never fails to interest restaurant owners and managers (and with good reason!). Although it is not difficult to teach yourself the different methods restaurateurs use to determine prices for their menus, you still have to find the process that's right for you. There is no single right way to price menus, but you can't veer too far off-base if you use the following five-step process:

Step 1.   Cost out your menu items. You must have a very good idea of your per-serving product cost for every menu product you sell. An item's cost should include the cost of the food, beverage, expected waste (such as meat shrinkage), other direct costs (such as plate garnishes and packaging used for take-out meals), and an allowance for indirect costs (such as table condiments and oil used in the deep fat fryers). There's a homemade recipe cost card software package on this book's Web site that you can practice on.

This is one of the most difficult things operators have to do, and it's easy to understand why they might tend to avoid costing their items. Purchase prices change often, and menu offerings change regularly. It takes a lot of time and effort (even in a restaurant that enjoys a sophisticated computerized management information system) to keep these costs up-to-date. It's easy to get lazy about this. Do not fall into that trap. If you do not want to keep up with the costs of everything you use in your restaurant, it's time to seek another career.

Some operators tend to fudge a little when costing out their menu items. For example, instead of considering the cost of every single ingredient used to prepare and serve a menu item, they calculate only the cost of the one or two most expensive food or beverage ingredients and use this information when pricing the item. Experienced operators who have worked every station in the restaurant can probably get away with this. Restaurants that have very predictable business may also have this advantage. However, few restaurants enjoy a great deal of predictability. And the novice operator will tend to price things too low or, worse, simply copy prices from a competitor's menu. The operator who has a firm grasp on the numbers will not make this disastrous mistake. Once you price something too low, you risk going broke before you can rectify the error.

Step 2. Multiply a menu item's cost by a factor of 3 to 7. If you are a value-oriented restaurant, then the multiples you use must be on the low side. The fancier your property and the more service you provide, the higher the multiple needs to be in order to generate enough sales revenue to earn a fair profit.

In some cases, you may find it advantageous to price an item using a multiple outside this range. For instance, if you want to move more wine, you might consider a multiple of 2 instead of 3. Alternatively, a low-cost menu item might support a very high multiple. For instance, a pasta dish with a selling price of $9.95 may cost you only about 95 cents, which is a multiple of about 10. The same might be true for postmix soft drinks, draft beer, and wine by the glass.

Use the highest multiple possible for the majority of your menu items, even with a bundling pricing strategy. Restaurants are voracious consumers of your cash; the labor and overhead expenses are huge. If your multiples are too low, you will need a superhigh, perhaps unrealistic, guest count to make up the difference.

If you are skittish about bumping up the multiples, come at it from a different angle. You can increase the multiple without it being obvious to your customers if you reduce your costs somehow—say, through more efficient purchasing and production. You might also consider altering a menu item's recipe somewhat by using substitute ingredients or trying a smaller portion size. If these options aren't feasible, you may have to drop the menu item, unless it draws a lot of folks who will buy other things.

Food-savvy restaurateurs with excellent business skills can unearth many little cost-saving opportunities that do not compromise the guest experience. A favorite story making the rounds a few years ago concerned the president of AMR Corporation (parent company of American Airlines), who found that removing one olive from each salad served to on-board passengers saved $40,000 a year. Similarly, the Hyatt Corporation discovered a while back that reducing slightly the number of strawberries in different dessert items generated close to a million-dollar savings in one year.

Step 3.   Check out the competition and compare your prices to theirs, but make sure that you are comparing apples to apples. Focus on direct competitors, especially those who operate in your trading area. You should also try to determine which restaurants among your competition have overhead expenses similar to yours. For instance, a restaurant that owns its real estate and doesn't pay rent or a mortgage, has a big advantage. Chances are, it uses somewhat lower multiples for pricing. However, if you simply copy these multiples, you could be signing your death notice if you are located in a high-rent district. There is always a tendency to underprice the items on the menu. Comparing your operation to one that enjoys a lower overhead compounds this problem.

Instead of comparing menu prices, compare the value you offer to that offered by the competition. While you may believe that you offer more value than a direct competitor, you can't carry significantly higher price points unless you operate in a unique environment, such as a tourist destination. You may be able to get a buck or two more, but you can't push it too much, unless you know for a fact that a particular menu item is wildly popular with your customer base and that guests can't get it elsewhere.

If you get too greedy, you're liable to give customers sticker shock. Don't allow this to happen, because if guests feel they are getting ripped off, they will not come back—and they will let their friends know about it.

Recently, a friend of ours went to a new ice cream parlor with her two small children. It was a very nice operation, definitely a cut above similar types of places. However, when she pulled out a $5 bill to pay for two children's-size cones, she was told that wasn't enough money. Like her, our first reaction to this story was, "Whoa!" That's a four-letter word you don't want to hear.

Step 4. Do a menu engineering analysis no later than one month after opening the restaurant and every quarter thereafter (see Chapter 5).

Step 5. Adjust your menu prices accordingly (see Chapter 5).

PRICING CATERING EVENTS

Private parties are the lifelines of many restaurants. They represent very predictable business, and, in most situations, they are very profitable. The more catering you do, the better your bottom line should be. Furthermore, catering sales revenue and profits can cover up many costly mistakes made in the day-to-day restaurant operation.

There are two pricing procedures that seem to work well.

Thirds Method

The thirds method involves calculating a price that will cover three things: (1) the cost of food, beverage, and other supplies (linens, dance floor, etc.); (2) the cost of labor and employee benefits to handle the function and the overhead expense needed to open the room (such as heat, light, and power); and (3) profit. A $30 price per person, for instance, would give you $20 to cover your expenses, leaving a $10 profit.

This method works very well when you build each party menu from scratch. Function hosts may like the personal attention received if you work with them to develop the menu, theme, and other event features. It takes a little longer to do this than it does to slap down a list of catering options, or your regular menu, and ask them to pick out what they want. But if you build the party from the ground up, it is much easier to account for every expense and guest need (such as a special diet). The resulting price, then, will cover everything; there will be no surprises.

This is not always the case if you use a standard catering menu. For instance, cost increases are harder to anticipate when you use a prepriced catering menu that you are committed to for a certain length of time. Furthermore, it is not very easy to determine the minimum number of guests needed to make the preprinted menu price work for you. When building the party from scratch, this isn't so much of a problem; once you know what the function host wants and the guaranteed guest count, you can add up the thirds, divide this sum by the guaranteed guest count, and present the price per person (plus tax and tip) for the function host's consideration. The quote given to the function host is very accurate; it can be either a price per guest or the total price for the party. Best of all, it is not a laundry list of charges; it is a bottom-line figure.

With prepriced menu options, you may have to include all sorts of other charges in addition to the menu prices, such as the rental of a dance floor, use of a disc jockey, or an open bar, because these menu prices don't cover them. Consequently, you'll have to dicker about each individual thing.

You may need to tweak the thirds pricing method on occasion—for instance, by dropping your profit third a bit in order to accommodate a good customer or one who you think will send profitable bookings your way in the future. Alternatively, you should consider bumping it up quite a bit if a guest wants you to close down the restaurant for the evening or if there is some sort of odd request that you don't feel comfortable with, such as the need to knock out a wall and rebuild it later. On the bright side, when guests ask for this type of accommodation, they are usually willing to pay big bucks.

Contribution Margin (CM) Method

The thirds method is the best way to price catering in the typical restaurant operation that does not serve a large number of private parties. However, if you have a large banquet hall and hope to do a great deal of catering business, it may be inconvenient to build each party from scratch. If you must offer prepriced catering options, and if you are willing to standardize what the guests can and cannot have, then the contribution margin (CM) method may be the better pricing option.

To use this method, you usually have to standardize everything, not just the menus. This can put you in the position of having to refuse some guest requests. You also must insist on minimum guest counts because it is not cost-effective to open a room or tie it up for only a small number of people. You cannot accommodate any surprises when prepricing the menus because your profit structure can take a big hit if you stray too far from the standard. The CM method will not work well unless you are in a very predictable environment and have a great deal of control over catering options. You have some leeway if you can charge exorbitant prices, but potential guests may avoid you if they think your prices are out of line.

This method also necessitates that you know as much as possible about the expenses associated with booking parties in your banquet room, apart from the types of menu items the guests will order. These are essentially fixed catering expenses, such as salaries and wages, utilities, paper products, and advertising, It is a good idea to calculate these types of expenses for a full year. It is also critical to keep these numbers up-to-date because your menu prices will be based on them. And keep in mind that, once you set the prices, you may have to live with them for a while.

These total fixed expenses must be divided by the minimum number of guests you expect to book for a year. This will give you a reasonable estimate of the amount of fixed expense per guest. To this, you need to add the per-guest cost for food, beverages, and other variables (such as special linen) that comes with a particular catering menu option. You now have an average per-person amount for all expenses.

Once you know how much the total variable and fixed expenses will be per person, add your profit margin to each menu option. This markup should be at least 75 percent. You need more profit than you might when you use the thirds pricing method because when you do a considerable amount of catering business, there will be more unpredictable overhead (such as unforeseen commissions paid to independent party planners). Furthermore, you need to cover any last-minute surprises. For instance, given the large catering volume, there will be more guest complaints; you will usually need to forgive part of the bill to rectify them. You cannot do this if your profit margin is too low, but you can be very gracious if it's high enough to begin with.

Let's assume that you have determined that all fixed expenses average $15 per guest to put on a party. Also assume that the variable cost of food and beverage associated with a particular menu option is $10 per guest. Your out-of-pocket costs are therefore $25 per guest. Add 75 percent profit markup, and the menu price becomes $43.75—say, $45 per person—plus tax and tip. If there are additional requests that you would grant to function hosts, and if these requests cost extra (e.g., charges for a dance floor rental), you must add them in or include them with the other variable costs before calculating the sales price.

The CM method can also be used to price the regular restaurant menu if the property has a very predictable customer flow. For instance, if you operate a facility inside a government building, you may know all your customers and what they like to order. You also may know when they will arrive and how long they'll stay. If so, the CM method is a viable pricing option for you. Do keep in mind, however, that the regular menu typically would not include such a huge profit markup.

PRICING FOOD AND BEVERAGE SPECIALS

A lot of restaurants today like to offer one or two specials for each part of the day. This is a good way to provide variety to guests without going through a complete menu revision.

Ordinarily, these menu items should be priced the same way you would any other regular menu item; you usually don't want to price them any lower. An operator may get a good deal on a food product or have leftovers to get rid of, so he or she puts out a special with a bargain price tag. But you have to be careful with this strategy because it can reduce your bottom line. If a customer who would normally order a Star menu item suddenly takes the bargain special, the gross profit (i.e., CM) for that guest plunges.

On the other hand, if, say, you have some very costly leftovers (such as 50 pounds of fresh salmon that is on the verge of losing its quality), cannibalization of a Star may be acceptable. Although you may reduce your contribution margin if a guest is diverted from a Star to the daily special, you might make up the difference by avoiding the need to toss out some expensive food.

PRICING ALL-YOU-CAN-EAT (OR -DRINK) MENU ITEMS

If you offer one or two all-you-can-eat (or -drink) options on your menu, they should be priced in the same way as any other item on your regular menu. The biggest difference is that, when costing out these menu items, you need to work with average cost figures instead of exact cost figures. When you first offer the item, you will have to estimate the average cost. Since this can be tricky, it is best to offer only a few of these menu items and only those that are inexpensive (such as soft drinks) and have the potential to draw customers who are likely to buy other things from you.

When you introduce one of these items as part of your regular menu, keep close track of how much of the food or beverage you use in the first week or two. This will help you gather enough cost and usage information to adjust the menu prices, if necessary, to bring them into line with your pricing requirements. Take a beginning inventory, add in your purchases of the relevant ingredients during this initial period of time, then subtract from this amount the ending inventory. This will give you the actual amount of food and beverage used during this time frame. Cost this out and divide the total cost by the number of guests who ordered this menu item, which will give you the average cost per guest. While this cost figure isn't as accurate as you might like it to be, it is better than guessing.

If you want to rely on guesswork, it's best to contact the purveyor of the particular food or beverage item and ask for a best guesstimate. For instance, the soft-drink vendor who services many restaurant outlets probably knows of a few restaurants that offer similar menu items and might be willing to share product cost and/or product usage information with you.

If you offer an all-you-can-eat buffet, salad bar, and/or breakfast bar option along with the regular menu, use the same approach to calculate the average cost per guest. This can be a little trickier when doing calculations for several such items, because, typically, there is a lot more waste. Options such as free soft-drink refills, or all-you-can-eat pasta or fish fry allow you to have more control. But food bars require special handling: you have to keep up their appearance, you have to rotate the items, and you usually have to discard things now and then that might still be edible but have passed their peak of quality.

PRICING MERCHANDISE

Logo merchandise can generate a few extra dollars, most of which is pure profit. If you're a unique restaurant, such as the Hard Rock Cafe or Planet Hollywood, you may actually make more money selling T-shirts than selling food.

Two of the main drawbacks, however, are the up-front charges you need to pay to develop the products and the large minimum quantities you usually need to purchase and store to get the best possible deals. For instance, the logo-imprinted bottled waters you sell for $2.95 apiece may cost you less than 30 cents per bottle, but you may have to pay several hundred to several thousand dollars up front to develop the proprietary label. In addition, you usually have to purchase several pallets, each one containing several cases, to get the 30-cent-per-bottle purchase price.

If you can absorb the up-front charges and the large amount and variety of inventories you must have on hand, consider buying and selling various kinds of merchandise. Guests love logo products. It's not unusual for them to get upset if you are out of a particular item that they made a special trip to obtain.

There are two typical ways to price these items. One is to include the product's cost when costing out a food or beverage menu item. For instance, specialty drinks can be priced using a very high multiple if you let guests keep the glasses or cups. The other way is to price them separately, after seeking the vendor's guidance. Vendors often have a sixth sense when it comes to pricing such merchandise. They know what customers are willing to pay. They also seem to know when you are getting too greedy.

PRICING SALES PROMOTIONS

Many restaurants like to offer pricing deals in order to generate more customer traffic. The idea is to get people to visit during normally slow periods or draw customers who will buy other, more profitable things. It can also be an effective strategy to help spread out your fixed costs over a wider customer base.

Diner's club options, two-for-one sales, early-bird specials, happy hours, and other forms of **discount pricing** are usually attempts to bolster business during times when you are open but have few customers (such as Monday

> **DISCOUNT PRICING Pricing deals in order to generate more customer traffic.**

evenings or from 4 P.M. to 6 P.M. on weekdays). If you can get guests interested in one of these deals, you then have a chance to sell them something else.

Discount pricing is controversial. In some competitive environments, it may be the preferred pricing method. However, even though it may generate customer traffic, what type of customer are you getting? Are you getting the "low rollers," who are looking just for the deal and nothing else? Are they more of a hassle than they're worth? Do they irritate your service staff, say, by tipping only on the discounted dollar amount instead of the full value? Do they irritate your steady customer base? Do they harm your reputation?

Things like the two-for-one dining program books sold by discount operators, such as www.dinnerbroker.com, seem to attract folks who would never go to your operation without the discount. They assume that they are paying what the product is worth and that all the other guests are overpaying. Furthermore, these customers are not loyal to your operation, nor can you expect to build loyalty among them. They are loyal only to the coupon book.

Folks purchasing discount books from, for example, the local high school band booster club, are not always this price sensitive. They realize that the purpose of the book is to raise money for a good cause.

Discount pricing can have many ramifications—one good, and the rest bad. If you start down this road, do it with your eyes open and be ready to commit to this strategy for the long haul. Once a patron uses a coupon and pays, let's say, 49 cents for a hamburger, psychologically this guest will never pay any more than that. The guest will visit you only when you are offering coupons. If you try to reverse the discount strategy, your business will drop. Once you get involved with discounting, it's hard to turn back.

Guests using coupons or visiting only during off-price times can also create security problems. If their coupons have expired or if the happy hour ends just as they come in the door, they will be mad. They may want to argue and put you on the defensive. Since it's never appropriate to argue with a guest, you will be forced to cave in and give them the discounted prices. Sooner or later, a coupon's expiration date and the happy-hour time frame may become meaningless.

If you want to offer pricing promotions, you need to first decide on the items to promote, as well as the times during which the promotion prices are valid. You then can use the **marginal pricing** technique to compute the menu prices.

MARGINAL PRICING A promotional method that allows you to earn a small profit by determining the price based on the cost of the product and other related variable expenses, plus a small profit markup.

Marginal pricing is a method that allows you to earn a teeny amount of profit. The technique requires you to determine the cost of the food or beverage product plus the cost of any other variable expense associated with selling that menu item. These other variable costs can be tricky to compute, since there aren't too many of them that are immediately apparent. For instance, you might consider allocating to the total cost of the price-promoted menu item a bit of labor cost. But if you already have staff in place, the labor cost may be fixed.

A good rule of thumb to use is to cost out the menu item and add a small markup to cover other variable costs needed to prepare and serve it. For instance, if you cost out a pasta dish at $3, add at least 10 percent, giving you a total variable cost of $3.30. This out-of-pocket cost is the lowest price you should charge if you expect to break even on that menu item. The price to charge, though, should be somewhere between $3.30 and what the price would be if you used the normal multiple. Say you normally use a multiple of 3 to price this menu item. If so, 3 times $3 gives you a $9 menu price. The price to your customer, then, should be somewhere between $3.30 and $9, say $6. Or you might go with a two-for-one deal, effectively pricing each meal at $4.50.

> **LOSS LEADER   A menu item on which you make only a small profit.**

> **LOST LEADER   A menu item for which you actually have an out-of-pocket expense.**

The idea is to price the promotions in such a way that you never go below your variable costs. It's one thing to offer a **loss leader,** on which you make only a teeny profit; it's something else to have a **lost leader,** for which you actually have an out-of-pocket expense. If you make a small profit, at least you have something built in that can be used to help defray the huge amount of fixed costs you have.

If everything works out, your overall income statement will show a bit more profit. The fact that you are creating extra business, even though it's not as profitable as you'd like it to be, nevertheless gives you a few more dollars to play with. The key word is *extra* business. If your pricing promotions merely reward existing customers who would normally pay the full price, you're in big trouble. If you suspect this is happening, you have to stop the promotions (if you can), go back to the drawing board, and research other possibilities that do not result in this problem. (See Chapter 9 for some good ideas.)

OTHER PRICING CONSIDERATIONS

There are some other things to consider when determining your price structure.

Daily Specials

If you offer daily specials that servers recite at tableside, make sure that guests are also told the prices. You don't want them to be surprised when the check comes.

Side Dishes

If you offer a menu item that in most restaurants customarily includes a side dish (such as a hamburger with a side of fries), but you want to price the side dish separately, make sure that the servers bring this to the guests' attention. For instance, servers should be trained to ask guests ordering hamburgers: "Can I bring a basket of seasoned fries, enough for the whole table to share? It's only $2.95."

Price Spread

In every menu item category listed on your menu, try to keep a reasonable spread between the highest price and the lowest one. There should be no more than a 100 percent spread. If, for example, the lowest-priced appetizer is $4.95, the highest-priced one should be approximately $9.95. If you want to serve an appetizer that has to be priced a great deal higher than $9.95, try to reduce its cost so that you can add it to the menu without throwing the category out of whack and scaring off customers. If that's not possible, list it on the menu at "market price." This allows you to serve it, but without advertising the price.

Take-out Items

If some of your regular menu items are popular with take-out customers, it might be necessary to raise the prices a little bit on these items. If you operate a quick-service operation, where take-out and drive-through business is standard, then the regular menu prices already take this into consideration. But if you have a table-service restaurant, it can be more costly to offer takeout, especially for items requiring expensive packaging. The expense of a phone ordering system may also need to be factored in, and there is extra labor involved.

On the other hand, take-out customers don't occupy tables in your restaurant, thereby allowing you to increase your guest count without a substantial change in your operating procedures. The key is to have a good idea of all costs involved so that the appropriate prices can be calculated. If necessary, print separate take-out menus to avoid any confusion.

Delivery Service

Delivery service is another way of increasing guest counts, but unless it is traditional for your operation to offer this amenity (such as a local pizzeria or a deli located in an office complex), you should approach this decision cautiously. Delivery can be a very unpredictable business. Staffing is a hassle. Insurance costs can be exorbitant. You usually must establish a minimum order. And it is necessary to restrict the delivery area.

If that isn't enough to scare you, quality control is almost impossible to maintain, forcing you to restrict the number and types of items you can deliver. Quality control is even more troublesome if you outsource the delivery function to an independent "waiters on wheels" contractor. If you don't mind taking the risk, there are ample rewards, as these types of guests are willing to pay a premium for the service, in addition to tipping the drivers. Your rewards will increase even more if you offer guaranteed delivery time or else the food is free—customers love this amenity. In fact, research shows that speed of delivery is the primary consideration when customers choose a delivery option.

Live Entertainment

If you occasionally offer entertainment in your restaurant, you may need to institute a cover charge. This is not necessary if all you offer is prerecorded background music. But if you feature live music on certain nights or on the weekends, you need to earn enough in cover charges to pay the band, defray related expenses (such as extra security and complimentary food and drinks), and generate a profit.

The easiest way to calculate a cover charge is to add up all relevant expenses and divide by the expected number of guests. Alternatively, you could capture this cover charge by establishing a minimum purchase per guest to give you the dollars you need to generate a sufficient profit. Say the entertainment expenses for one night are $1,000, and you expect to serve 250 guests. A straight cover charge would be $4 per guest just to break even, and more than $4 per guest to generate a little extra for the house. But in lieu of this cover charge, you might require guests to purchase a minimum of two drinks at slightly inflated prices—if you normally charge $3 per drink, ask for $5 per drink. This strategy has higher profit potential because some guests will order more than the minimum number of drinks.

Corkage Fee

Some guests want to bring their own beverages (usually wines) with them when they visit a restaurant. If the alcoholic beverage commission in your area grants patrons this option, you need to decide whether you will allow your customers this privilege. If you do, you must determine how much you need to charge guests for handling the product, providing the drink setups, and generating a profit.

This is a touchy issue. On the one hand, guests know that they will have to pay something. On the other hand, guests who bring their own alcoholic beverages tend to be quite sophisticated and so are very aware of what a standard corkage fee should be. If you charge a corkage fee, you must research what other restaurants charge. If you are not in the same ballpark, you will alienate these guests.

Realistically, corkage fees can't be that high. You must hope that by allowing guests to show off their personal wine cellars, they will reciprocate and purchase a lot of highly profitable dishes from you. In fact, if many of your guests bring their own wines, consider bumping up the multiples you use to price the food menu items. A slightly higher food menu price is more palatable to such guests than a corkage fee that generates the "whoa!" response.

THINGS TO DO TODAY

- Ask the soft-drink route salesperson for pricing suggestions.

- Find out what the corkage fee is at the best upscale restaurant outside your trading area.

- Cost out a new recipe and determine its suggested menu price.

---

http://tca.unlv.edu/profit

7

SERVICE: HOW DO I GET MY STAFF TO GIVE THE RIGHT AMOUNT OF ATTENTION?

Managers do not control the quality of the product when the product is a service. . . . The quality of the service is in a precarious state—it is in the hands of the service workers who produce and deliver it.
Karl Albrecht, coauthor of *Service America*

Like many retail operations, the restaurant industry is unique in that employees are part of your product. When managers think of marketing, they usually think of advertising, personal selling, and other efforts directed toward potential customers. But a restaurant's *first* marketing efforts should be directed internally, to employees.

Employees are your internal customers. They must be excited about your restaurant and the items on your menu; otherwise, it

will be impossible for guests to become excited. Good vibes stem-
ming from the staff will infect the guests. When they visit your operation, they will be happy. It will then be up to you and the staff
to keep that happiness meter in the positive zone.

External marketing brings customers into the restaurant, but
does little good if the service delivered by the employees does not
meet or exceed guest expectations. The food in a restaurant may
be outstanding, but if the service person has a poor attitude or provides inattentive service, customers will feel dissatisfied and down-
rate the overall restaurant experience. They won't care how great
your food is; without good service, it is nearly impossible to create guest satisfaction.

Richard Normann, author of *Service Management,* coined the
phrase "moments of truth." A **moment of
truth** occurs whenever employees and customers come into contact. Normann states
that when this occurs, the company no
longer directly influences what happens. It is the skill, motivation,
and other tools employed by the server, merged with customer expectations and behavior, that create the service experience.

> **MOMENT OF TRUTH When
> employees and customers
> come into contact.**

When employees and customers interact, a careless mistake by
an employee or an unanticipated request by a guest can result in
guest dissatisfaction. Your job as manager is to help employees eliminate mistakes and prepare them to meet customer demands. To do
this, you need to create a service culture by hiring employees who enjoy customer service, and training them in ways to avoid mistakes
and how to recover when mistakes do occur, thus providing them
with the tools they need to succeed. In essence, you are motivating
them to give 110 percent.

Poor service can cause guests to leave and never come back. In
an article posted on www.cnn.com, Deborah Feyerick commented
about a study conducted by Feltenstein Partners, which concluded

that approximately 7 percent of casual restaurant customers and 12 percent of upscale restaurant customers will not return to a restaurant that gave them lousy service. This tells us that restaurants with poor service can expect higher customer churn, which you want to avoid as much as possible.

Other studies have shown that if you can increase repeat patronage by as little as 5 percent, you can increase your profit by as much as 25 percent. Moral of the story: By increasing service quality, restaurants can increase repeat business and become more profitable.

Service creates a memorable event for the guest. In an article in *Nation's Restaurant News,* Clint Clifford stated that, when focus groups of restaurant customers are asked to recall memorable experiences, they almost always talk about the employee who went out of his or her way to help them. Great service creates profits for the restaurant and fond memories for the guest.

COMMUNICATING WITH AND MANAGING YOUR CUSTOMERS

In a restaurant, the employee and the guest interact with the service delivery system. Just as your employees do, your customers become part of your product. Consider a couple who selects a restaurant because it is quiet and romantic. However, a group of loud and boisterous conventioneers is seated in the same room, disrupting their intimate dinner. This couple will be disappointed in their overall experience—that is, they will be disappointed in your product. To ensure excellent service, you must manage customers in such a way that they do not create dissatisfaction for other guests. In this example, seating large groups away from other guests or in a private room would have minimized the negative interaction.

Another opportunity for negative interaction crops up whenever there are small children as guests in a sit-down restaurant.

Managing this situation might call for providing games and other diversions to keep the children busy and minimize disturbances to other guests.

Since they are coproducing the service, customers and employees must understand each other. They also need to understand your service delivery system. For example, customers must understand the menu to ensure that what they order will meet their expectations. If customers do not know what "al dente" means, they may send back their "uncooked vegetables." Employees should be able to anticipate when a guest needs an explanation about a particular menu item.

Think through the entire service delivery process and identify where problems might occur. A case in point is the "doneness" of meat. A restaurant manager noticed that a lot of steaks were being sent back. She discovered that a "medium" steak means different things to different people—some people expect it to be pink in the center; others expect that they will see no pink color. Thus, "medium" is an ambiguous term. Smart operators will define their terminology, either on the menu or by having the service person explain the restaurant's definition of such ambiguous descriptions. If a guest expects a pink center in his medium steak, the server must ascertain this from the guest and communicate it to the kitchen staff, thereby ensuring guest satisfaction.

MANAGEMENT COMMITMENT: A PREREQUISITE FOR GOOD SERVICE

Management must be committed to the service culture. If you expect employees to exhibit a positive attitude with guests, you need to present the same attitude to your staff. You must live it and breathe it. This is the only way to guarantee consistent quality of service.

Stay away from the one-shot deals that some managers use to pique their employees' enthusiasm. A lot of organizations waste money hiring trainers to come in for a day to excite their customer-contact employees about providing high-quality customer service. The effect of these sessions is usually short-lived because the organizations do little to support the servers and other customer-contact employees over the long haul.

The best way to ensure a positive attitude on the part of the staff is for the owner/manager to prowl the property on a daily basis, monitoring the level of enthusiasm. Not only does this communicate that the owner/manager is excited about the business, but that excitement trickles down to the rest of the staff.

Why is it that when a new manager takes over a business, the sales revenue often changes quite a bit? It's not unusual for a new manager to precipitate a significant sales revenue spike as well as a big jump in the happiness meter. The explanation is that the new manager approaches the job with a service mentality, understanding that to make money in this business you need to fill the dining room, not hide out in the back office, poring over the accounts.

Management must, therefore, develop a **service culture:** a culture that supports customer service through policies, procedures, reward systems, and actions.

> **SERVICE CULTURE** A culture that supports customer service through policies, procedures, reward systems, and actions.

A service culture is part of the **organizational culture,** which is the shared values and beliefs that give your employees direction about how they are expected to behave. In well-managed companies, everyone in the organization embraces the service culture. A strong service culture gives your employees a sense of purpose and makes them feel

> **ORGANIZATIONAL CULTURE** The shared values and beliefs that give your employees direction about how they are expected to behave.

good about your company. Your employees will know what you are trying to achieve and how they are helping you reach that goal.

Developing a customer-oriented organization requires a commitment of your time and financial resources. The actions of management are one way that an organization communicates with its employees. Management at all levels must understand that employees are watching them for cues about expected behavior. If the general manager picks up a piece of debris off the floor and throws it in the trash, others will start doing the same. A manager who talks about the importance of employees working together as a team can reinforce the desire for teamwork through personal actions. Taking an interest in employees' work, lending a hand, and knowing employees by name are all part of a good service culture.

Good managers treat employees and customers with respect. They discuss service with their employees, and they ask what they can do to help them provide better service.

In *Nation's Restaurant News,* Ron Yudd remarked that the service-based leader is always in service to others within the organization. He or she acts as a tool giver so that others can get their jobs done while simultaneously exceeding their own expectations. He states that making sure others have the tools to get the job done is the hallmark of a service-based leader. This type of manager sees to it that there are enough plates, iced-tea spoons, Solo cups, carryout packs, linen, and so on. He or she also continually provides information and training that will make it a pleasure for employees to take care of their guests.

The best way to keep service timely and consistent? Ask yourself everyday, "How can I help my servers do a better job?"

IF YOU WANT FRIENDLY SERVICE, HIRE FRIENDY EMPLOYEES

The accepted wisdom is that not everyone has an aptitude for service. If you want to offer friendly, courteous service, you must hire friendly, courteous people. Sounds simple, doesn't it?

Restaurant managers often comment that good service comes from the heart. Excellent servers care about their guests and get a good feeling when they see customers enjoying their dining experience. They work hard at anticipating guest needs, realizing that this is a difficult task because all guests are different.

It is almost impossible to train people to be friendly and care about others. You can train employees to perform the technical skills needed for good service, but you will usually be frustrated if you attempt to train them to be friendly and caring. You must find people who come on board with these traits. Unfortunately, there aren't enough of these folks to go around.

Everyone is looking for high-quality employees, which means you need to make a serious effort to recruit servers who already have positive attitudes and friendly personalities. The recruiting and hiring process requires a great deal of time and effort; however, in the long run, it will be more cost-effective than scrambling to repair service mistakes made by poor employees.

Chef/restaurant owner Charlie Trotter feels that "an individual's attitude is the most important consideration" when he hires someone. All excellent owners and managers seem to agree on this, so you have your work cut out for you.

To identify a positive attitude, you have to find out as much as you can about a prospective employee's personality. One possibility is to present the person with a few unusual customer service scenarios and ask how he or she would resolve them. You could also ask creative, probing (but legal) questions whose answers would shed some light on the candidate's personality—for example, "If you were an animal, what kind of animal would you like to be?"

An innovative recruiting tool for restaurants interviewing several potential servers in a group is to involve one or two customers in the process. The customers can share their insights and opinions. They can also tell you the kinds of attributes they like their servers to possess. Ideally, you'll be able to find employees who possess them.

In *Grassroots Marketing for the Restaurant Industry,* author Adam Berringer states that customers look for the following traits and behaviors in servers:

- Greets guests at the table or counter, or on the phone, with a smile

- Makes customers feel at ease

- Can answer questions about menu items

- Knows the restaurant's policies and procedures

- Qualifies the customer for the sale

- Shows appreciation for the customer's business

One subtle recruiting tool that many restaurant operators don't think about is the external marketing program. External marketing is done to attract customers, but it also helps to attract employees. Russ Bendel, president of Mimi's Café, noted in a recent *Nation's Restaurant News* story that one key to attracting employees is to become an employer people really want to work for. Bendel stated, "It's important to be an employer of choice, a cut above all the rest, a place where you are creating opportunities and a chance to grow professionally and personally."

When you have a solid external marketing plan that enhances your operation's brand image, a side benefit is the good feeling potential employees have about you. In their minds, you are an employer of choice. How sweet it is when job candidates start knocking down your door.

GOOD SERVICE REQUIRES PRODUCT KNOWLEDGE

Once you've hired your employees, you must train them. Employees should be given information about the company's history, its current businesses, and its mission statement and vision. They must be encouraged to feel proud of their new employer. You want to instill in them a desire to contribute to the company's success.

In well-managed restaurants, service employees know the menu inside and out. They are trained to direct guests to menu selections that will best suit their tastes. They are also taught how to sell menu choices to guests who haven't made up their minds yet.

Every restaurant should conduct tastings, where employees sample the products they are selling. Product training is a continuous learning process; it should be part of every company's employee training program. Properly trained employees are confident employees who deliver consistent quality service. This enhances your image and attracts more guests and potential employees to the operation.

Another aspect of training that the restaurant industry needs to emphasize is convincing employees to respect their jobs. Instruct servers in the importance of this position and the contribution it makes to the restaurant. Communicate your expectation that they will treat the job seriously, not just as something to do until a "real" job comes along.

Bernard Martinage, of the Federation of Dining Room Professionals, discussed these issues in a recent edition of *Nation's Restaurant News,* commenting, "Service is 20 years behind the evolution of cooking here. A cooking career was not looked at in a glamorous manner until now. Service needs to be viewed in the same way."

Tim Zagat, of Zagat restaurant surveys, believes that many restaurateurs—such as Rich Melman, Danny Meyer, and Wolfgang Puck—are already sensitive to the need to professionalize service and give it respectability. He is optimistic that other restaurant managers will follow suit and that, eventually, restaurant service will become a respected profession. Use your training programs to enhance the server image. Do your part to make it a more respected profession. This will help you attract and retain good employees.

Some managers ask why they should spend money training employees if these employees are just going to leave. This thinking is influenced by NRA statistics revealing that limited-service restaurants have an annual employee turnover rate of over 100 percent, and that full-service restaurants are close, with a rate that approaches 90 percent. But this negative attitude can turn into a self-fulfilling prophecy by creating unnecessary employee turnover. If the employees are not properly trained, they are incapable of delivering the appropriate service. Being unable to deliver good service, they will lack confidence. The resulting stress will sooner or later drive them to quit. Unfortunately, quitting reinforces employers' beliefs that they should not waste their time and money on training. Not investing in employee training programs leads to a cycle of high employee turnover and guest dissatisfaction. You can break this cycle; in fact, you need to see to it that it doesn't even begin in your operation.

A part of your training program should be devoted to **upselling.**
Give servers the tools they need to increase

> **UPSELLING   Training servers in methods to increase the average check.**

the size of the average check. For example, servers and counter workers should be taught to ask customers if they would like an appropriate accompaniment with their order. Asking people ordering take-out pizza whether they want to take along a bag of seasoned bread sticks for just a buck more can make a substantial difference in your bottom line.

To help servers, and to ensure that they don't forget something when they are rushed, you can purchase computer technology that prompts them with specific options to relay to guests. For instance, when a cashier rings up a meal order, the computer screen will show some suggested side items to recommend to the guest.

This software can also determine the amount of change a guest is getting back and prompt the cashier to offer the guest another item for the amount of that change. For example, if a guest is receiving 60 cents in change, the computer will prompt the cashier to offer another sandwich for 60 cents. This may be less than the regular menu price, but when offering it as an add-on purchase, you can afford to take a little less profit. It's money you wouldn't get otherwise, but just by asking, you might get the guests to leave their change behind. It's not free money, but it's the next best thing.

The most sophisticated form of upselling is called **consultative selling.** It's relatively easy to practice up-selling, especially if you have a computer to prompt you. But consultative selling can't be practiced unless the server understands his or her customers so that appropriate recom-

> **CONSULTATIVE SELLING**
> Training servers to increase the average check and enhance guest satisfaction.

mendations can be made. It is much more than just blurting out, "You want fries with that?"

Certain restaurant customers dine out frequently, enjoy wine, and have the money to buy the best. They are open to suggestions, and money is no object. Consultative selling in this case comes from knowing a lot about good wines and the particular wines the restaurant has available. You will need to find someone well-versed in this area to serve this type of customer. However, there are other customers who want a good wine but are price-sensitive. In this case, consultative selling involves the ability to recognize this customer expectation and suggest an acceptable, moderately priced wine that will make them happy.

Here's a dessert example. If a couple seems hesitant about dessert, the server could probe a little by asking whether the guests have eaten their fill, whether they would like something light to go with their after-dinner coffee, or whether they have an off-menu request. If they reply that they're stuffed, the server can suggest that they share a dessert, which will enhance the couple's meal satisfaction, while simultaneously increasing the amount of their check.

Upselling focuses on increasing the average check. But consultative selling has a dual purpose: it focuses on both increasing the restaurant's average check and enhancing guest satisfaction. It's a subtle difference, but an important one.

GOOD SERVICE ALSO DEPENDS ON FAIRNESS

Rules and rewards that reinforce customer service should be established. Your challenge is to develop rules and rewards that will support the delivery of good service.

For example, service stations must be stocked ahead of time in order to serve customers properly. However, some servers don't like to come in a half hour early to restock and set up the dining room, believing that it's a poor use of their time since they don't receive tips during this period. If these servers are allowed to come in late and avoid side work, the responsible servers will become upset at the inequity and might eventually resign. You will then be left with employees who do not care about your business or your customers—and who may not care much for you, either.

You must treat your staff evenhandedly in order to create a motivated team to which everyone contributes his or her fair share. In conversations we've had with servers over the years, it's clear that they lose their motivation quickly if they think a manager is being unfair. For example, an employee who requests time off on a day that's usually very slow, but is consistently refused, will undoubtedly perceive this as unjustified.

One server occasionally requested Tuesdays off so she could help her son's Boy Scout troop. But she never got this day off, even though every time she requested it she was told it would not be a problem. Another person complained that the manager gave preferential treatment to his favorites. These kinds of actions can cause negative vibes and lead to unnecessary employee turnover. To motivate your employees, rules and policies must be applied equally and enforced across the board.

Recognizing employees who provide exceptional service lets them know that you appreciate them, as well as their professionalism. Employee-of-the-month awards for front-of-the-house and heart-of-the-house employees are a good way of acknowledging superior effort. They work even better if the award includes a little monetary incentive.

A good way for a company to reward employees is to hire a mystery shopping service to visit the restaurant and look for servers who go beyond the call of duty. When the mystery customer finds an excellent server, he or she is given a cash award right on the spot. When Patti Shock did mystery shopping for the Cozymel's restaurant chain, she carried a $50.00 gift certificate in her purse and was told to give it to the server if he or she told her table about all of the daily specials, including menu prices. Instant reward; instant gratification.

Contests also work well as part of your reward system. They don't have to be elaborate. They can be something as simple as giving a dinner for two to employees with perfect attendance throughout a particular month.

Some restaurants develop contests to make work more interesting and to create a competitive spirit. These contests might focus on things like determining the fastest server or the most acrobatic bartender. They could also be structured around nonwork themes, such as finding out who is the best golfer. Mark Farmer, director of marketing for Sonic, once remarked that he felt the company's reduction in employee turnover was partly due to these types of contests and games.

Reward systems can backfire and create resentment, so take steps to prevent this from happening. For example, if you run employee contests, offer several levels of prizes for each contest so that more than one person can be rewarded. Keep in mind that, if you use rewards sparingly, they won't become stale and predictable, thereby losing their effectiveness.

There are risks involved with any reward system, but they can also be an effective means of recognizing—and retaining—good employees.

COMMUNICATE WITH YOUR EMPLOYEES

Employees should receive information about promotions that you'll be running in the future, so they have an idea of what to expect and what their role will be. For instance, before you place a promotional advertisement in the newspaper, show it to your employees and explain the purpose of the ad.

Beth Lorenzini of *Restaurants and Institutions* states: "Promotions designed to generate excitement and sales can do just the opposite if employees aren't involved in planning and execution." She uses an example from Lawry's The Prime Rib to illustrate her point.

Lawry's increased its Thanksgiving Day sales by 48 percent through employee involvement. Management invited all the wait staff to a Thanksgiving dinner a week before the holiday. They were served the same meal that they would be serving guests on Thanksgiving Day. Not only did the dinner become a festive affair, it got everybody into the Thanksgiving holiday mood. It also provided an excellent lesson. Employees knew exactly what was going to be served on Thanksgiving Day, including wines that went well with the meal. Management also asked the staff for suggestions that would make the promotion run smoothly.

Like the employees at Lawry's, your staff should be informed about promotions. They should hear about promotions and new products directly from you, rather than having to read it for themselves in advertisements meant for external customers.

RECOVERING FROM SERVICE FAILURE

A recent study we conducted on complaint behavior found that very few customers who had complaints would take the time to record them on customer comment cards. They voiced their dissatisfaction either to a manager or to an employee, or they would leave without saying anything. And if they leave without registering their complaint, they rarely come back.

Our study uncovered several types of complaints, the primary one being slow or inadequate service. Almost one-third—31.6 percent—of the respondents complained about this. Overall, the major sources of customer complaints and the percentage of persons voicing them were as follows:

Slow/inadequate service	31.6 percent
Improperly cooked food	11.5 percent
Poor value	11.1 percent
Rude/unfriendly service	10.6 percent
Noise/loud music	7.5 percent
Cigarette smoke	6.0 percent
Lack of cleanliness	5.0 percent

Only a little more than half (58 percent) of those surveyed complained when they had a problem. This means that almost half of those customers experiencing a problem don't complain; they just leave and seldom return.

If complaints can be resolved, the majority of the complainers will come back. Getting customers to voice their complaints, so you have a chance to fix the problem, is an opportunity to increase your profits.

Another interesting finding of this study is that guests indicated they were more likely to complain if they felt their complaints would result in a positive resolution. Guests who felt the restaurant would not care about their problems left without voicing their dissatisfaction. Conclusion: It is important to encourage customers to complain. Create an atmosphere where customers feel comfortable bringing problems to your attention.

Employees should be trained to listen and respond to complaints. Managers should be empathetic and work out reasonable resolutions to complaints. Better yet, you might consider training and **empowering servers** to fix problems then and there, instead of having to tell guests, "I'll get the manager."

EMPOWERING SERVERS
Training employees to handle problems on their own, without the manager.

Company policies and communication practices can be used to encourage complaining. For example, offering a satisfaction guarantee or noting on the menu that if the food or service is not satisfactory, the customer should let the server know are two ways of encouraging customers to complain.

If unhappy guests leave without voicing their complaints, they may never return to the restaurant and they spread negative word of mouth. When customers in our study complained about a problem and had it resolved to their satisfaction, 64 percent stated that they would return to the restaurant. In turn, these customers would relay a positive message about the restaurant to an average of three other people. This is in contrast to guests who complained but didn't receive satisfaction; they won't come back, and, worst of all, they passed along negative word of mouth to at least six other people.

These figures demonstrate that it is important to give customers an avenue for complaints and to do as much as is humanly possible to find satisfactory resolutions to their problems. When done successfully, complaint resolution will achieve its two main goals: getting the customers to return and encouraging positive word of mouth.

We highly recommend *A Complaint Is a Gift*, by Barlow and Moller, which notes that many managers pay mystery shoppers to patronize their restaurants and evaluate the food and service. The drawback of using these shoppers is that, often, they are not part of the restaurant's target market—they do not represent the restaurant's typical customer. But a person with a complaint *is* a typical customer. Furthermore, the customers who are most likely to complain are your best ones. They are telling you something is wrong with your operation because they want to come back. They want assurance that you will take care of the problem and things will be back on line during their next visit. You should appreciate the fact they are giving you a chance to fix the problem. Listen up and respond. Mystery shopping services charge money for their services; a complaint is a gift.

A lot of operations use customer comment cards, e-mail, and/or toll-free customer comment lines to gather complaints and figure out how to resolve them. These are okay, but there are better solutions. You should develop real-time complaint resolution policies. Customer comment cards, e-mail, toll-free numbers, angry letters, and so forth, are not the most effective way to solve most problems. They may be an excellent way of gathering useful information, but they do not provide what most guests want: a quick resolution.

INVOLVING AND MOTIVATING EMPLOYEES

Managers must constantly work at keeping employees motivated. An effective technique for enhancing motivation is to involve employees in decisions that affect them. This gives them the opportunity to buy in to the decision, and it also provides you with valuable information about how a given decision might work out if it were implemented. Involving employees in the decision-making process and developing tactics to enhance their motivation keep them interested in their jobs.

This process can be a little risky, but if you take a few precautions, it can be a useful management technique for you. Lay out the ground rules from the start, and let everyone know that you will be the one to make the final decision, after taking into consideration their input. This way, your employees realize that you're going to control the end result, but they are generally satisfied that their own issues received a hearing.

The following case illustrates why it is beneficial to seek employee input when making managerial decisions. A manager decided

TIPS FOR CREATING GOOD SERVICE

- Create a service culture within your organization.

- Ask how you can help the service staff do a better job.

- Base your hiring decisions on attitude.

- Include information about your company values in your training program.

- Conduct food tastings for employees regularly.

- Train servers to acknowledge customers when they first enter, when they are seated, and when they leave.

- Identify and resolve communication problems that exist between guests and servers. Don't take anything for granted.

- Train servers to stay on the floor when they are not busy, instead of retreating to the back of the house.

- Train servers to anticipate guests' needs without interrupting them. If water glasses are low, fill them automatically rather than asking the guests if they would like more water.

- Train servers to communicate with guests; they especially should let them know how their meals are progressing in the kitchen.

- Train servers in complaint resolution.

- Train servers to let guests know you appreciate their business and to invite them to come back.

- Tell your employees about promotions that are being communicated to your external customers.

- Create self-directed employee teams to enhance service and employee motivation.

- Manage the emotional side of your workforce.

to install a new computer system in his restaurant. This was in the early days of the technology, and the system was a first-generation product. In this system, the guest checks had to be marked with a pencil. The computer would read the marks, send the order to the kitchen, and then spit out the bill.

The manager did not bother to consult with his employees before installing this system. In fact, the employees did not know it was being installed until a short time before the dining room opened. All the servers immediately resisted the new computer system. They were quickly frustrated with it. They did not receive proper training, and, what's more, they did not see any added value from using it. They perceived that it would result in extra work, service slowdowns, and all kinds of other problems.

One server discovered that the machine was sensitive to butter and other grease marks, which it read as pencil marks. To demonstrate their frustration, servers intentionally smeared their hands with grease before handling guest checks. The end result was that customers received wrong orders, as well as erroneous checks. The servers blamed it on the new system, and, in fact, the customers sided with them; they, too, disliked the computerized service. Less than three weeks after it was installed, the system was removed from the restaurant.

Involving these employees in the decision-making process might have helped gain their support for and interest in learning the new technology. The manager could have tried selling the idea by emphasizing the system's benefits and innovations. Excluding the employees from this process resulted in resistance to the change, as well as a big drop in their motivation.

Another decision-making area where managers should involve employees is uniform selection. Uniforms make employees easily identifiable and create the impression that they are accessible. Uniforms play a role in the atmosphere that a restaurant creates, and they can contribute greatly to guest satisfaction. They advertise your professionalism.

Choice of uniforms will influence employee attitudes. Employees dressed in formalwear feel and behave differently. A research project conducted by Professor Kathy Nelson and John Bowen found a significant relationship between employees' perceptions of their uniforms and their overall job attitude. If an employee rated the uniform high, he or she also had a very positive attitude toward the job.

Management often looks for uniforms that reflect something about the business. They are considered one of the operation's marketing tools, something to enhance the restaurant's image. That's fine; however, it is critical that you solicit employee input regarding function and projected image.

For example, food servers at a pirate-themed restaurant complained about the loose-fitting sleeves on their shirts and blouses. The uniforms looked great until the servers began working. The sleeves dragged across plates when they were being cleared or when trays were being unloaded at the dish machine. After an hour or two, the sleeves were stained with food. This embarrassed the employees when they approached guests. Thus, they became less outgoing while serving. When choosing a uniform, consider its practicality—for example, does it have pockets?—as well as how comfortable it is to wear.

A touchy situation arises when some employees think the uniforms are overly revealing. A good compromise is to keep this uniform, but assign an employee committee to help you develop an alternative that meets your needs and expectations. You can then let each server decide which one to wear. Even if you don't want to use the committee approach, you could accomplish much the same result by asking your vendor to design two or more acceptable uniforms and let each server select one that meets his or her personal needs. This approach has been successfully used for cocktail servers in Nevada casinos.

It is very important to consider employee concerns when selecting uniforms. Involving the customer-contact employees who will be wearing the uniforms in your decision can be a win-win situation.

In *W.O.W. 2000,* Barry Cohen describes how the Olde San Francisco Steakhouse company develops self-directed work teams to keep employees motivated. One of the teams is the Contest Team, which develops employee contests that are simultaneously fun and motivating. Cohen states that the contests are designed to be a team affair, for example, pairing a less experienced server with a more experienced server.

The Olde San Francisco Steakhouse uses other types of teams as well. The Business Recognition Team takes wine and cheese to local businesses as an introduction to the restaurant. The Recognition Team makes sure good employees are acknowledged, by using such techniques as handing out thank-you notes to servers spotted giving excellent service or throwing an anniversary party for a long-term employee. The Scheduling Team helps create the service staff work schedule, considering factors such as who gets the best station and who works the closing shift.

The team concept gets employees involved, gives them a voice, and keeps them motivated. Cohen says these teams "are a high touch way to reward people every day, and even more importantly, to allow people to initiate positive change without the participation of management." He believes these teams make employees more interesting and more fun to be around, which can only help your business.

In addition to doling out the motivators, you must also eliminate conditions that zap motivation. For instance, some guests can be difficult and even abusive. Employees often find it hard to manage their emotions in this type of situation, and self-control becomes even more difficult if the employee is tired from working a long shift

---

OATH FOR TODAY

Service is one of the most important elements of my product mix. I can and will control the level of service provided. I will make a serious effort to provide good service and will use it to differentiate my restaurant from the competition. People may steal my recipes, imitate my ambience, or use the same food purveyors, but they cannot recreate my service culture. Service culture is a journey that never ends. I am ready to take that trip.

or overtime. Having sufficient staff so that servers need not work more than 40 hours a week results in better service and fewer mistakes.

Overworked employees are tired, which means they probably don't have enough energy left to care about their customers. Most of us have either been in that position ourselves or been the victim of an overworked, emotionally drained server. Enthusiastic, well-treated employees provide good service; tired workers don't. Schedule sufficient staff on each shift and do not overwork your staff if you aim to provide good service.

Most owner/managers learn early on how to manage labor costs, develop work schedules, put together staffing guides, and so forth. Add another task to this list: managing the emotional health of your workforce. It's the best way to ensure that your servers present a positive face to your customers.

THINGS TO DO TODAY

- Locate a copy of the book, *Service America*, and make sure to read it.

- Next time you go out to eat, ask the server what ingredients are in the dish you want to order.

- Brainstorm a contest with your service employees. Then implement it.

---

http://tca.unlv.edu/profit

8

OTHER INCOME STREAMS: HOW MUCH EXTRA STUFF CAN I SELL?

While most restaurant revenue stems from the day-to-day food and beverage sales, there are many other opportunities to gain extra income. The major opportunities within most operators' reach are catering, delivery service, take-out service, and merchandise sales.

Before deciding to take advantage of these opportunities, let us warn you: don't do it unless your core business is solid. If your core business is shaky, shore it up before you decide to develop new lines.

If you develop new lines of business, choose ones that will be a good fit with your existing operation, and make sure you can do them well. For example, an off-premise catering event should reflect favorably on your operation and motivate people to try out your restaurant. A cold meal that is supposed to be hot, served unprofessionally by someone who has forgotten the salad dressing, may have just the opposite effect—it can drive people away from your restaurant and create negative word of mouth.

Another thing to consider, if you get involved in ancillary income streams, is to be sure that the production, service, and administrative systems needed to support them are well planned, designed to accommodate the extra sales, and well executed.

CATERING

Every day, thousands of business and social groups sponsor gatherings attended by hundreds of thousands of people. Most of these functions involve food and beverage. Restaurants with function space or the ability to cater off-premise can benefit from these events.

On-premise catering requires space for private functions. Some restaurants have small private dining rooms. These rooms are ideal for events such as small business meetings, wedding rehearsal dinners, board meetings, and committee meetings.

If you are designing a new restaurant, you can enhance your revenue capabilities by including several small rooms. If they are designed properly, these rooms can be opened up to serve as normal dining space when there are no special functions on the books. If you have entertainment or lounge space that is not used during the day, this space may also be suitable for group events. Groups that utilize catered events include businesses, social and fraternal organizations, reunions, religious organizations, meeting planners, and wedding planners.

To help you list potential customers for your catering service, locate a membership directory from the local chamber of commerce. This is a good place to begin your journey into the world of catering because it gives you information about its members, including the all-important contact information. Armed with these data, conduct a direct-mail campaign, following up by phone, to determine which member organizations hold receptions, banquets, or luncheon meetings. Try to schedule a personal visit to explain your services to those you have qualified as regular users of outside caterers.

Catered events require business procedures that are different from those of normal restaurant operation. (For an in-depth guide to this specialized field, refer to *On-Premise Catering*, by Patti Shock and John Stefanelli.) From a marketing standpoint, you will need to develop catering menus. Looking at the catering menus of your competitors might be a good place to start, but yours will usually have to be structured around your regular restaurant menu, since you already have the systems in place to produce these menu items.

When putting your menus together, avoid including items that you cannot prepare and serve well. Also eliminate those that are not practical for large groups.

Some restaurant operators are under the impression that they cannot compete effectively with the big hotels and country clubs for catering business. This is a misconception. In reality, restaurants usually can be more competitive because they do not have the huge overhead expenses of larger facilities, and they often can be more flexible. There is also less red tape for clients to contend with. Furthermore, since catering is add-on business for you, you can afford to negotiate more freely.

One of the primary requisites for a profitable catering operation is a contract, with a required deposit and guarantee. A common mistake that new catering services make is to fail to enforce these requirements. The biggest offense is not charging clients for the guaranteed number of guests, but only for those who show up.

A typical guarantee policy is for the client to pay for the guaranteed number of guests, even if the actual cover count is less. The restaurant usually agrees to produce up to 5 percent over the guarantee, and to charge extra for each guest above the guaranteed number.

Here is an illustration of the importance of the **guarantee.** A manager was able to turn an unprofitable catering operation into a profitable one, simply by enforcing the guarantee. The previous manager had a policy of charging only for the number of guests who showed up, which meant that the restaurant had labor and food charges but no compensation if the number of guests fell below the guaranteed count. It also meant that, most of the time, the events were over set, since there was no penalty if the client overestimated the number. Enforcing the guarantee put dollars in this manager's pocket, in addition to putting the pressure back where it belongs: on the clients. Clients soon learned to forecast attendance more carefully.

> **GUARANTEE An arrangement between client and restaurant, whereby the client pays for a guaranteed number of guests.**

This is a common problem. As part of their education, many students in our college are required to plan, organize, and implement catering events. Getting people to agree to guarantees can be a real headache. Clients seem to think that, since they are dealing with a school, there should be some flexibility because money is not the paramount concern. If, for instance, an organization guaranteed 50 attendees, but had only 45, the client simply paid for 45 and couldn't understand why we went out of our way to collect for the other 5. Good management practices are at the heart of the education these students are getting, and learning to be firm about guarantees is an essential lesson for anyone considering the catering business.

Getting into the catering business requires additional staff training. For instance, anyone who answers the phone at your restaurant must be knowledgeable about the catering options you offer. He or she should be able to answer any sort of questions that potential clients might ask or be able to refer clients to someone who can answer their questions.

You should designate only one person to be responsible for booking the events, and this person must have a thorough understanding of the difference between regular restaurant sales and catering sales. Among other duties, he or she will have to work with clients to develop menus, put together a list of on-call servers, and develop outside sources for things such as equipment rentals, entertainment, dance floors, florists, and balloon artists.

The *special events coordinator* needs to understand how the typical client thinks. For example, clients expect you to ask them for the event date; however, many don't have an exact date in mind, so they will quote dates around the time they would like to hold their events. If you are flexible (which, compared to the typical hotel or country club, you *are*), you can work around the clients' needs. But if you are unable to accommodate a requested date, always suggest alternatives. Don't let clients get away that fast! If a client's date is not flexible, at least find out whether the event is an annual one, so that you can make contact next year. You should also find out whether the client holds other events that you might be able to handle.

The special events coordinator also should be a good price negotiator, with thorough knowledge of the restaurant's pricing structure. Pricing can be tricky in that you often must price events on a case-by-case basis. (See Chapter 6 for some suggested pricing procedures.)

Restaurants that lack space for on-premise catering events may still be able to create revenue from off-premise catering. Like on-premise catering, off-premise catering can be very profitable. Many executives, for example, like to entertain in their homes, but do not want to have the burden of preparing and serving the food and drinks and cleaning up after the event. They are often willing to pay big bucks to have you do this for them.

Off-premise catering is a unique and complex segment of the restaurant industry. It is even more unpredictable than the on-premise business. Off-premise catering can require additional equipment (which has to be stored somewhere!), such as outdoor grills, food warmer carts, and tents. It requires you to be exceptionally well organized. If you forget the salad dressing when you are catering an off-premise event, it is not just a matter of going back into the kitchen for it—you have to make a trip back to the restaurant or to the nearest grocery store.

DELIVERY

An alternative to off-premise catering is delivering food to your customers. Delivery allows customers to enjoy your food without coming to the restaurant. It also eliminates the service requirements of off-premise catering.

Restaurants located downtown or around office parks can increase lunch sales by delivering to offices. Office staff often prefer having food delivered rather than taking time to go out. A lot of businesses have working lunches; it's more efficient for their employees to eat in.

Distributing flyers promoting your delivery service to these offices is a good way of getting the word out that you deliver. Every now and then, your staff should take tastings around to the offices during the middle of the afternoon, along with flyers about your delivery service. This is an excellent way to promote your delivery service.

Pizza restaurants earn a good portion of their sales from delivery. But any restaurant can capture additional sales from offering this service. You may not even need your own drivers. In most towns, there are food delivery services. For example, in the Seattle area, 2Go Services delivers food for over 20 restaurants. They charge the customer a delivery fee and charge the restaurant a commission.

A typical restaurant should be able to sell at least 50 more meals a week through the addition of a delivery service. Many restaurants sell hundreds of additional meals a week through delivery services.

Preparing meals for delivery or takeout isn't the same as doing this for your dine-in customers. First of all, you need to have someone available who is trained in taking delivery orders. This order taker must know enough to ask the right questions, such as finding out how customers want their food prepared and what sauces or condiments they want.

Delivery also requires having disposable containers that fit the image of your restaurant, keep the products fresh, and control the temperature of the food during delivery.

Once you get organized for delivery, doing your own or signing an agreement with a delivery service can be a good source of additional income. There is a potential downside, though (see Chapter 6).

TAKEOUT

Take-out business is driven by convenience. Most delivery and take-out customers use these services because they want the convenience of having someone else prepare their meals.

Some customers don't want to pay extra for delivery. They would rather pick it up themselves. Making it easy for them to pick up and pay for the food will help your restaurant take advantage of the lucrative take-out business.

For instance, Chili's has several reserved parking places near the front door for customers to use when picking up their orders. Outback Steakhouse even sends someone out to the customer's car with the food—drive-through service, Outback-style.

If customers must enter your restaurant to get their orders, make it quick and easy for them to pay, pick up, and go. On busy days, you should have someone specifically assigned to expedite this activity. If the process is too slow, your future in the take-out business is questionable.

Jennifer Mann, writing in the *Kansas City Star*, notes that Applebee's brings in over $10 million a year from its take-out sales. The company views take-out sales as a great way to increase same-store sales. In fact, corporate management has developed a strategic initiative to increase this business.

Foodservice operations in office buildings and hospitals are realizing they can enhance sales by developing prepared meals that are purchased by office workers on their way home. When these customers get home, all they have to do is reheat the meal and serve it.

Customers for take-out service are primarily people who are time-poor—in other words, they do not have a lot of free time. If you can provide a solution that will save them some precious time, you can create sales.

Families in which both heads of the household work outside the home are time-poor. There will be days when neither parent wants to cook, but they do not want to round up the family and go to a restaurant. They prefer the convenience of dining in the comfort of their homes.

On occasion, couples without children and singles also do not want to prepare food, but prefer not to dine at a restaurant, either. Their often hectic work schedules may necessitate that they frequently eat out with clients and other business associates. During their leisure hours, they just want to veg out in front of the TV. Take-out meals are ideally suited for such customers.

Some folks in your target market may have unique needs that can be satisfied with your take-out food. A story in *Food Service Director* described how a foodservice manager discovered that many people in his office building took off for Long Island after work on Fridays. So he sold them picnic baskets to take along on the trip. During the summer months, the baskets accounted for an additional $1,000 in business each week.

In fast-food operations, take-out service can account for over 70 percent of a restaurant's volume. Takeout accounts for about a third of the typical pizza restaurant's sales volume. A casual sit-down service restaurant can increase sales revenue by 5 to 10 percent by offering a take-out service.

Takeout and delivery can be excellent ways to increase sales revenue and provide added value to your target market. However, if these services are not well thought out, they can disrupt your operation and result in poor service for both the off-premise and the on-premise customer. Before you jump into this, make sure your operating systems can handle the extra business.

For many restaurants, takeout is *extra* sales revenue that you derive from your current customers. You usually don't have to expand or retrofit your existing facilities to implement it. Best of all, takeout can easily add three to four points to your bottom line.

MERCHANDISE

Ah, merchandise—what an angle! You get people to pay for the privilege of advertising your operation. And, in most cases, they pay handsomely. People who talk about exorbitant catering prices don't seem to mind paying huge prices for a few trinkets.

Most restaurants have hundreds of people going through their doors each day. Some have thousands. Selling additional products to them can bring in additional profits. It can also help promote your restaurant.

Restaurants sell over 700 million T-shirts each year. This generates several billion dollars in annual profits and creates 700 million walking billboards. In some restaurants, merchandise sales account for as much as 50 percent of total restaurant sales revenue.

Most restaurants have an opportunity to increase income by selling merchandise. Some may limit this to gift certificates. Others, like the Hard Rock Cafe, may offer an extensive line of merchandise that can bring in as much revenue as food and beverage sales.

The first step in starting a merchandise program is to figure out the type of merchandise that will fit your operation. A restaurant in a tourist area can provide logo wear that serves as a souvenir, an upscale restaurant may provide bottles of its sauces, while a coffee bar can sell coffee mugs and cups. Neighborhood taverns often sell logo T-shirts, sweatshirts, and baseball caps to loyal patrons. Restaurants with successful merchandise operations sell products that complement their businesses.

Some restaurants sell merchandise that encourages guests to remember enjoyable experiences. This is particularly true for some of the biggest beneficiaries of the merchandise sales trend: entertainment-theme restaurants, such as Planet Hollywood, Harley-Davidson Cafe, House of Blues, Hard Rock Cafe, and Hooters.

Doug Manago, vice president of merchandise for Hard Rock Cafe, stated in a recent *Restaurant Business* article that "most of our merchandise has the city name on it. The company did research to find out the viability of cross-selling merchandise from other restaurants in their shops and found that customers had no interest in buying merchandise from Hard Rock Cafes in different cities. They wanted souvenirs from the city they were in and the Hard Rock Cafe they were visiting." His research illustrates the souvenir value that logo merchandise can have to tourists.

A popular merchandise opportunity for restaurants catering to travelers is peg games. Po Folks, a casual restaurant near Knott's Berry Farm and Disneyland in the Los Angeles area, caters to vacationing families. To keep the kids occupied while they are waiting for their food, the restaurant provides games the kids can play with their parents. For those who enjoy the games and would like to have their own set, Po Folks sells them at the cashier stand.

In some restaurants, merchandise has become an integral part of the product. Cracker Barrel restaurants, for instance, are designed so that everyone who enters the restaurant must pass through the gift shop. The Country Kitchen takes that approach a step farther. Since the restaurant doesn't take reservations, customers usually must wait for a table. Although the restaurant provides a small waiting lounge, the logical thing for customers to do while they wait is to browse the adjacent gift shop, which is stocked with Pennsylvania Dutch–style curios.

Bakery products have become a popular addition in some restaurants. The bakery section does more than add extra profits. When placed in the entrance, it provides tangible evidence of the restaurant's food quality. In fact, managers of restaurants selling bakery products claim they are a great way to promote your core food and beverage items. This contention is supported by research summarized by Dan Malovany in the trade paper *Bakery Production and Marketing*. The study found that 50 percent of a casual restaurant's customers would visit more often if the restaurant added a bakery.

Consider Marie Callender's Restaurant and Bakery. Customers entering the restaurant are exposed to the sight and smell of freshly baked pastries, which gets them thinking about dessert and take-out options. Best of all, it assures them that they are in for a pleasurable dining experience. The strategy works. The company sells millions of pies a year. Some of the company's restaurants sell a thousand pies a day. Pies bring people to the restaurants. Pies are excellent impulse items. Who could leave Marie Callender's without a pie?

MERCHANDISE MANAGEMENT

Like other areas in the foodservice operation, to be effective, a merchandise program must be properly executed. What might work for a food promotion may be ineffective for merchandise. There's more to it than simply putting a few logo items on display, sitting back, and raking in the money.

David Farkas, writing in *Restaurant Hospitality*, shares this anecdote about purchasing a baseball cap in a restaurant. "It's inside a glass case with some other stuff that's got the restaurant's logo on it. But no one's around to take my dough or give me the cap. The hostess spots me and says she'll call a waitress. When one finally shows up, she says she has to go to the manager's office, where the merchandise is under lock and key. She vanishes before I can tell her to forget it. She returns (cap in hand), takes my money, and disappears again to make change."

Think about it. A customer is begging the operator to take his money. But somehow, baseball cap sales have become an afterthought in that operation.

Farkas's experience is exactly the wrong way to market restaurant merchandise. Jim Makens and John Bowen discuss the right way in an article in the *Cornell Hotel and Restaurant Administration Quarterly,* which notes that there are three steps to creating an effective merchandise sales program in a restaurant:

1. Select the right merchandise.
2. Match the merchandise with the location.
3. Create merchandise excitement, making it easy for customers to buy.

The Right Stuff

Selecting the right merchandise is an obvious first step to merchandising success, yet the choice of what to sell is sometimes made haphazardly. All merchandise buyers need product guidelines that provide direction without restricting creativity. This is as true for a family-operated restaurant as it is for a chain.

Price points, differentiation, and assortment define the product mix.

Decisions concerning **price points** (i.e., the range of prices of-

PRICE POINTS The range of prices offered.

fered) that will appeal to your customers directly influence all other aspects of merchandise sales. Pricing decisions must be made according to the target customer, the restaurant's image, and profit goals. Family restaurants, for instance, should provide a selection of low-priced (though highly profitable) gifts. Specialty restaurants, on the other hand, can successfully sell products that might seem overpriced. (See Chapter 6 for some suggested pricing procedures.)

Robert LaFrance, writing in *Forbes,* shares this example from Matsushia, a popular Beverly Hills Japanese restaurant. Michael Cardenas, the manager of Matsushia, says, "Our customers are high-end people who could get a New York Giants cap at Joe Blow Sports shop for $10. We sell ours for $20 and customers don't mind." Anybody for $30? Is America a great country, or what?

Price-point determination should always be a matter of policy rather than being left to the individuals who do the purchasing for your operation. Excessive variations in your price points could quickly become unmanageable and confusing to customers in the absence of clearly defined guidelines.

As niche retailers, restaurants must carry highly differentiated merchandise. Attempts to compete with mass-merchandise or specialty chains on the basis of price would be foolhardy. You should stay away from merchandise retailing if you are unwilling to support continuous new-product acquisition with a creative and knowledgeable buyer. For example, the creative person who does your purchasing might dream up a way to sell locally made products, such as handicrafts and specialty prepared foods. This strategy ensures product differentiation and keeps new products coming on line all the time. It can also generate community support for the restaurant.

Some restaurants have achieved **product differentiation** by putting dates or locations on merchandise. The Black Dog Tavern on Martha's Vineyard prints a dated T-shirt annually, making each year's shirt a collector's item. Restaurants with multiple locations, such as Planet Hollywood and Hard Rock Cafe, print the location of each restaurant

> **PRODUCT DIFFERENTIATION**
> Differentiating merchandise in order to create uniqueness and enhance profits.

on their T-shirts. Customers collect the shirts from different locations around the globe.

Maintaining the breadth and depth of a product line is usually a challenge for restaurants because of space limitations. Consequently, operators often incorrectly elect to offer a wide assortment of merchandise, but provide little depth in their product lines. This inevitably creates cluttered merchandising and inventory problems, such as stockouts and difficulty with restocking.

Stockouts are especially irritating—and costly. If you're out of an item, it's tough to convince the customer to come back for it later. Merchandise sales are often impulse buys. Once the guest leaves, odds are that he or she won't come back.

Customers can get very upset if you are out of an item they want to buy. The irritation meter hits the red zone if customers have promised friends and relatives back home that they will buy these things for them. The meter is in the double red zone if customers have made a special trip, waited in line, and discovered that the item they want is out of stock.

A few years ago, the assistant controller of the Mirage Hotel/Casino in Las Vegas, which had recently opened, was a guest speaker in one of John Stefanelli's classes. He remarked that the company thought it had a good handle on logo merchandise. But early on, it became very clear that everyone seriously underestimated the demand for these things. People complained about stockouts and were quite upset when they couldn't get the desired item. The hotel/casino had to scramble. Managers decided that, until they could revamp the merchandise sales program, they would take disappointed guests' names and addresses and send the items to them at their homes, at cost, in order to maintain customer goodwill. For good casino customers, the company sent the stuff out at no charge.

If space is a problem, you're better off offering a few products—say, polo shirts and baseball caps in two or three colors—and maintaining a large inventory. This approach simplifies inventory control, may earn large-quantity purchase discounts, and will improve the merchandise display appearance.

Matching Merchandise and Location

Product merchandising and real estate ventures share a common success factor, namely, location. The decision of where to locate items involves determining where to put product groups and then arranging the best placement of individual products.

The location of products depends largely on the restaurant's design. In most cases, existing restaurants were designed with no thought given to merchandise sales. Design specifications for new restaurants increasingly demand careful consideration of product location to ensure sufficient space.

A restaurant's entrance or waiting area is a logical location for merchandise. Correct **product location** is a reflection of a basic marketing principle: you must continuously study and know your customers. Few restaurants face the complex customer traffic pattern of a super-

> **PRODUCT LOCATION**
> Determining where to place merchandise to achieve best sales.

market or discount store. Observation and discussion with the staff can generally answer questions such as, "How long do customers remain in an area?" and "In what direction do most customers turn?" You usually don't need a sophisticated study to tell you such things.

Some other operations, however, may not find the issue to be so clear. For example, Harley-Davidson, Hard Rock Cafe, and Planet Hollywood, after careful consideration, decided to imitate their retail neighbors by opening separate retail merchandise outlets that can be

---

THOUGHT FOR TODAY

Entertainment-theme restaurants have drawn the industry's attention to merchandise sales, but the opportunity is not limited to these high-profile operations. Most restaurants can profit from some form of retailing. To be successful, select the right merchandise, match the merchandise with an appropriate location, create excitement, and make it easy for customers to spend their money. And don't forget to manage it as closely as you do your food and beverage operations.

accessed through the restaurant, as well as directly from the street or the shopping mall.

If customers won't come to you, why not go to them? Think about putting together a great, interactive Web site (see Chapter 10) that will complement your in-house efforts. A lot of restaurants are using the Internet to sell their products. Once you have established a solid merchandise sales program on-property, expanding to the Internet is the next logical step. After all, you don't want to leave any money on the table if you can help it.

The Internet is a great option for customers who occasionally want to order something for themselves. It's an even better option for those who want to order gifts for others. No doubt about it, the Internet can leverage your sales revenue and profit potential.

If tourists make up a substantial portion of your target market, a Web site is a must. Tourists can't visit you very often, but that shouldn't stop you from making it easy for them to spend their money. A good example is Cheeseburger in Paradise, a popular tourist spot on Maui, which has an Internet site for its merchandise.

If you've been in business a long time, chances are that many of your former customers have moved to parts unknown. But you can find them through the Internet. For example, Dunkin' Donuts developed an Internet site to sell its coffee. One of its target markets is customers who have moved away from the East Coast to areas where Dunkin' Donuts does not have outlets. These customers love their Dunkin' Donuts coffee and (here's the best part) are willing to pay a premium to have it shipped to their homes.

If product sales fail to meet revenue and profit goals, the merchandise sales strategy must be changed. Alterations must be made in the product line (i.e., the right stuff), price points, and/or location. It's natural to focus your attention on the first two, but don't forget about location. It's easy to assume that the reason for poor sales is that the product line is tired. But it could be that the physical location for your merchandise sales is lousy or that your Internet site is not effective.

Excitement Plus

Probably the best way to generate enthusiasm for your merchandise is to develop attractive **point-of-purchase (POP) displays.** Daniel Bendall stated in *Restaurant Hospitality* that display cases near the front of the restaurant can increase sales of these items significantly. The reason: POP displays stimulate **impulse purchases.**

> **POINT-OF-PURCHASE (POP) DISPLAYS** Placing merchandise in high-traffic areas, typically located next to a cashier stand.

For example, Farrel's Restaurant in Hawaii serves a clientele composed of families with young children. Recognizing this, the pathway to the cashier's area was re-designed to become "candy and toy heaven," heavily larded with hundreds of irresistible impulse items. Jim Makens reports that his informal interviews with management indicated that the program added 10 percent to the bottom line.

> **IMPULSE PURCHASE** Something bought on the spur of the moment. An unplanned purchase.

Perkins Family Restaurants is another chain that realized the potential of placing POP displays in the cashier area. Perkins features high-margin pastry items in multitiered displays next to the cash register. Guests can't miss them. The inside of the glass counter serves as a focal point, or what marketing gurus refer to as a "customer stopping tactic."

OTHER INCOME POTENTIAL

Here are some other things you can do to pick up a few extra dollars:

1. *Supplier rebates.* When you purchase anything, there are usually some opportunities to qualify for some sort of discount. There are quantity discounts, volume discounts, cash discounts, new-product-introduction discounts, freight-damaged-goods discounts, demo-model discounts,

salvage buys, used-equipment sales, going-out-of-business sales, and so forth. If you know what you're doing and have the cash to back your play, you can earn a nice chunk of change.

2. *Grease sales.* You can sell your used grease and other related items, such as fat trimmings from meat, to salvage companies who recycle them into things like cosmetics and fertilizer. Not a lot of money in it these days, but there could be enough to interest you. In earlier days in the business, it was common for the executive chef to keep the money generated this way. It was considered a job perk.

3. *Other salvage income.* If you don't mind the hassle, you could gather up your empty cans, cardboard boxes, glass bottles, and so on, and sell them to a recycling outfit. Like grease recycling, this is not a big deal today. In fact, in some parts of the country, it's the other way around: you have to pay people to haul the stuff away. Generally, though, aluminum cans are still worth your trouble. The original MGM Grand, in Las Vegas, had one person in charge of collecting all recyclables, including the empty aluminum cans, and delivering them to the recycling center. Net profit from this venture: over $100,000 per year, most of it from selling the aluminum. (And this was more than 20 years ago.)

4. *Interest income.* Banking and investment geniuses might take the time to juggle the cash accounts in order to squeeze out every little bit of interest income before they have to pay their bills. This could result in some serious money for a large restaurant. Since you usually collect from guests long before you have to pay for the things they consume or the employees who produce and serve, the bucks can add up.

5.   *Advertising income.* Some folks will pay you in exchange for advertising on your menu or in your operation. For example, you may be able to earn some sort of promotional discount from vendors who are allowed to plug their products. A particularly creative example is the type of advertising The Cheesecake Factory sells. Its menu looks like a book, with right-hand pages listing menu items and left-hand pages displaying ads for all kinds of things.

THINGS TO DO TODAY

- Find out how much it costs to have logo caps made for your restaurant.

- If you have a friend in the retail merchandise business, ask him or her to give you an idea or three that might work for your operation. (Don't forget to comp your friend's meal!)

- Call the local recycling center and find out how much it's currently paying for empty aluminum cans.

---

http://tca.unlv.edu/profit

9

COMMUNICATIONS: HOW DO I GET ON THE GUEST'S RADAR SCREEN?

A restaurant operator is both a promoter and a communicator. When you promote your restaurant, you are giving people reasons to visit your operation. You can communicate your message through paid media, such as newspapers, magazines, radio stations, and television stations. Or you can use free sources of media, such as publicity and positive word of mouth. Both can be effective, but the free ones are almost always more effective than the ones you purchase. People know you can say almost anything you want in your ad; thus, they tend to put more stock in what a neighbor or a restaurant reviewer says about your restaurant than what you say in an ad.

This chapter will give you some very specific ideas about how to promote your restaurant using paid and unpaid methods of communication. It will also explain the importance of planning this communication. After reading this chapter, you will be able to reduce or, better yet, eliminate ineffective promotions and replace them with cost-effective techniques.

PROMOTION DOs AND DON'Ts

There are various issues to take into account when considering the implementation of a promotion strategy.

Make Sure Your Product and Service Are Strong

Many of us don't think about promotions until we notice a drop-off in sales. When sales decline, managers generally decide they need to promote their restaurants in order to turn this trend around. But this will have disastrous results if the reason for the sales drop is poor food, service, or cleanliness. In a nutshell, if the value you offer isn't working, fix it. If your restaurant is not competitive, spending money on promotion will put you out of business. It will bring in customers who will be exposed to your problems, resulting in negative word of mouth.

The number one rule of promotion is that, before you even think about implementing one, your product and service must be strong and consistent, and must be perceived by your target market as better than your competitor's, or at least unique enough to draw favorable attention. If you don't have a competitive advantage, you'd better develop one before you start throwing money around on promotions.

Promotions Work If You Give Them a Chance

Promotions work! Some managers spend thousands of dollars promoting their restaurants, yet they remain pessimistic about their possibility for success. These managers behave as if the money they spend is wasted and will have no effect on sales.

For instance, a manager might spend a considerable amount of money on a two-for-one promotion, but keep the same level of staffing and purchase and prepare the same quantities of food. This manager is taken by surprise when customers respond to the promotion and start pouring into the restaurant. The manager is then forced to scramble, often in vain, to try to provide good products and service in the undersupplied, understaffed restaurant. The customers who try the restaurant because of the promotion will never return, and some will even spread negative word of mouth about it.

When you implement a promotion, assume it will work and ramp up for the extra customers it will bring you. Effective promotions create satisfied customers, who will return to your restaurant and spread positive word of mouth.

Use Promotions to Change Customer Behavior

Promotions should be designed to change behavior. You don't get any points for having the prettiest ad or other promotional piece. The whole purpose of a promotion is to get customers to do something they are not currently doing. This could be getting them to come more often for dinner during the week, buy an appetizer with the main course instead of buying only a main course, or attend a special event.

In designing promotions, some managers fail to see them as a means to change behavior; they just promote. For example, a Mexican restaurant in a residential area had a good weekend dinner business, but lousy weekday dinner business. To correct this, the operator started promotions featuring a two-for-one dinner coupon with no restrictions. The restaurant, which previously had short waits on the weekend, now had waits of more than one hour. You can guess what happened. Those customers without coupons left, because they could go to any restaurant and pay full price—there was no incentive for them to stay. But the coupon holders stayed. The outcome of the promotion was that almost all of the weekend dinner customers were paying a portion of their bills with coupons. The customers who would have paid in full left, and many did not return. The restaurant closed its doors after a few months. If the manager had planned a promotion that would bring people into the restaurant when the business was needed, he might still be around today. Instead, not only did the promotion bring in unneeded business, it drove away the best customers.

Make a Plan

Promotions must be planned just like any other business function. For example, managers routinely develop work schedules, par inventories to help with purchasing, and daily food production schedules based on past history. But the purchase of media to promote the restaurant is often a knee-jerk reaction to low sales volume or a pesky salesperson's pitch.

You need to plan media purchases ahead of time. You would never buy a food product without researching it a little bit or at least trying out a free sample. You should take the same approach when buying media exposure. For a new restaurant, the plan might involve testing different types of media, such as newspapers, radio, or the Yellow Pages, and then selecting the most effective ones. For a going-concern restaurant, the manager can also develop a contingency plan to implement during slow periods. However, this type of plan should include an investigation into the reason that sales are off, so that problems can be fixed before placing a promotion in the media that are most effective for your type of operation.

Without a plan, you can expect to end up spending money on ineffective promotions. For example, a salesman selling a directory of restaurants approached a restaurant manager in Dallas. The salesman explained that the directories were being developed for hotels in the area and would be used by travelers to select restaurants. The salesman showed the manager a directory that contained advertisements for the restaurant's competitors. He then offered a special deal because there were only two spots left and he wanted to close out the directory. The salesman's pitch was convincing, and the manager paid hundreds of dollars for one of the spots. The manager later found out that his competitors' ads were simply clipped from other media and pasted in the directory; none had paid for a spot. The manager also found out, after talking to some local hotel managers, that their hotels had actually been paid to receive boxes of the directory; whether they distributed them or recycled them was their choice. Most of the directories were never placed in hotel rooms. Even worse, the restaurant manager was unable to track any sales to the directory.

Now if this manager had had some kind of promotional plan in mind, he never would have considered purchasing a spot in an unfamiliar directory. To avoid such directory scams, stay away from those that have no track record. Tell the salesperson that, if the directory is still around one year from now, you will consider buying a spot. Chances are, you'll never hear from that salesperson again.

Target Appropriate Media

The costs for exposure in various media are based on the amount of people exposed to them. One implication of this is that if all the people exposed to your ad are not in your trading area, you are paying for exposure that has no benefit. For example, if you are an individual restaurant in a major city, you may find that 80 percent of your customers live or work within five miles of your restaurant. If you advertise in the major city newspaper, you will be paying for many readers outside your trading area. This is why chains usually come into a market area with three or more restaurants. The restaurants collectively will cover much of the population, which makes it cost-effective for them to purchase such media advertising.

A key aspect of media planning is to look at what might work based on your restaurant's trading area. For example, to promote lunch business, the manager of Theodore Zinck's, a downtown restaurant, passed out flyers on sidewalks near the restaurant. Hundreds of people who passed within a block of the restaurant during the lunch hour were potential customers. As most of these folks resided or worked in the trading area, this proved to be an inexpensive, yet effective, way of promoting the restaurant. Restaurants in high-traffic areas often use this technique to enhance their business.

You need to understand which media create the most value for your restaurant. You should occasionally conduct surveys, based on time of day, that ask for customers' home zip codes, where they work, where they are coming from (work or home), and which media they watch, listen to, and read. Match the media (e.g., newspaper, radio, magazine, television) your customers like and use with the geographic area they are coming from when they visit your restaurant, the geographic coverage of these media, and the cost of the media. By doing this, you can eliminate the media that your customers don't care about, as well as the media that extend beyond your trading area.

Develop a Promotion Budget

A promotion plan should include a budget, which should be based on what you want to achieve, not on how much spare change you have in your pocket. If, for instance, you target tourists, you will need to use constant marketing, because you have to bring in a new set of tourists every few days. You will get repeat business from loyal guests and referrals from satisfied customers, but you must continually draw first-time visitors. Your promotion budget will have to take these expenses into account.

Established neighborhood restaurants may be able to get by with meager promotion budgets, so long as they have a loyal customer base. For example, the Tillerman, in Las Vegas, does very little advertising. Over the years, it has built up a loyal following, and these people promote the Tillerman through positive word of mouth.

But it is the rare operator who does not have to spend any money on promotion. Sooner or later, every company will lose customers. Some move away, and, even in the best-run restaurant, some customers will experience an unresolved problem. In well-managed restaurants, the customers brought in by positive word of mouth may be enough to offset customer churn. But in most restaurants, positive word of mouth needs to be supplemented with promotions in order to maintain acceptable customer counts. In this case, the amount budgeted for promotions will depend on the degree of customer churn. A well-managed restaurant with great food and service needs less promotion than a mediocre restaurant. You can get a lot of mileage from just a few promotion dollars if you develop and maintain a strong, consistent product and service package.

A promotion budget should be based on what you want to achieve and not on an average dollar amount that restaurants in your class spend. You must determine very specifically what you want to accomplish. Approach each promotion as an investment. You need to know how much the promotion will cost and approximately how much profit you expect to earn.

For example, an existing operation wants to develop a three-week promotion plan that will add 50 covers a day to its weekday lunch business. Assuming an average check of $20, if the promotion is successful, it will bring the restaurant approximately $15,000 of additional sales revenue during the promotion period. This will generate an additional contribution margin of about $10,000. Furthermore, you can expect to convert up to 20 percent of these new customers into repeat patrons, resulting in a long-term sales revenue increase. If this three-week promotion costs less than $10,000 and achieves its objectives, it will produce a tidy return on investment.

If you think your promotion budget may be a little too rich for you, consider using **trade-outs** to reduce it. Many media will accept these in lieu of cash payment. For instance, if your restaurant is a suitable place for an advertising account executive to entertain clients, you may be able to

TRADE-OUTS A promotional arrangement allowing you to pay with products or services in lieu of cash.

trade restaurant meals for advertising space. This is a great deal because it allows you to leverage your promotion budget significantly. If your advertising bill is, say, $500, and you pay with $500 worth of meals, your out-of-pocket expense is only about $200. In most trade-out arrangements, you can buy at least twice as much ad space for your dollar. However, this type of deal is only good if the media you purchase zeros in on your target market and covers your trading area adequately.

TYPES OF PROMOTIONS

A restaurant manager can use a number of promotional tools. These tools include **advertising, sales promotions, personal selling, database and direct marketing, loyalty marketing, public relations, local area marketing,** and **word of mouth.**

One of the problems we notice with unplanned or poorly planned promotions is the use of only one or two of these options. The well-planned, successful, cost-effective promotional campaign will include all relevant types of promotions. It will also include as many types as possible in order to maximize synergy.

Advertising

Advertising is the term used for communication that you pay for in order to place it in a media outlet. It includes newspapers, magazines, directories, radio, television, and the Internet.

ADVERTISING Communication that you pay for in order to place it in a media outlet.

When purchasing advertising it is important to have sufficient frequency to ensure that your target market will be exposed to it long enough to remember your spots. Studies have shown that small amounts of advertising are not effective. The level of advertising must reach a critical mass before you will begin to see a positive return on your investment. Independent restaurateurs often try out a one-shot ad to see if it will be effective.

Most of the time, a single ad will not be effective, and the manager concludes from this that advertising is a waste. But to be effective, not only does advertising have to be planned, it also needs to be run with enough frequency to create an impression with your target market.

Newspapers Newspapers are a good way to reach local customers. The planning time for newspaper ads is short, but you should always plan far enough in advance so you have enough time to proof your ads. For most papers this means you need to place your ad a week to ten days before it runs in the paper.

Larger restaurants and chains can afford advertising agencies to help them design their advertisements. Smaller restaurants often rely on the newspapers to design the advertisements for them. In both cases, you should provide the agency or the newspaper with a clear idea of what you want to achieve and whom you want as the audience for your message.

Sketch out the design for the advertising layout. Often, local newspapers will do a better job of designing an ad for a small restaurant than a major paper in a large city. This is because a local or neighborhood paper will view a small restaurant as a potential regular advertiser. Thus, it has the potential of becoming a major account. If a local paper designs an ad for you, ask for the slicks of the artwork so that you can place them in other media placements.

When arranging for a newspaper advertisement, think carefully about where in the paper you want to place it. Many restaurants place their ads in the entertainment section, because they know that those planning an evening out will turn to this section. However, if your ad is tied to a sporting event, such as Monday Night Football, you need to be in the sports pages.

When you use printed media, you should develop a message that has a singular focus. Advertising is expensive, so some restaurant managers try to squeeze as much as possible into their ads. These ads are often confusing and tend not to attract the attention of readers.

The average person is exposed to over 1,500 advertisements per day. If your ad is going to be one of the few that gains a customer's attention it needs to be well designed. For example, if you want to promote luncheon specials, design an advertisement whose headlines will attract those who dine out at lunch. The message should be composed to tell them about the benefits you offer, persuade them to come to your restaurant, or remind past customers why they should return for lunch.

Newspapers charge for ad space by the column inch. The rate per column inch will depend on how much space you agree to purchase in the coming year. Thus, planning ahead and signing a contract can lower your cost per ad. Before committing, though, check the penalty charge for not using the agreed-upon amount of space. Most newspapers will simply go back and charge you the difference in price between your contract rate and the rate you would have been required to pay if you hadn't signed an annual contract. In this case, there is no risk involved in signing the contract.

Some newspapers offer a national rate to companies, like McDonald's, that have outlets throughout the United States. This rate is usually higher than other rates because all of the readers exposed to the ad should have an opportunity at some point to make a purchase from a national company. If you are a local franchisee, you need to make sure you are being charged the local rate and not the national rate.

Some newspapers will have higher rates for ads featuring entertainment. If you advertise live entertainment, find out whether there is a special rate for ads that mention only entertainment. If there is, consider advertising the entertainment separately from a food or beverage special, thereby creating two smaller ads that might save money.

Magazines Magazines offer better-quality graphics than newspapers, and they have a longer life. Many people may keep a monthly magazine in their home for one to three months. Thus, an advertisement in the May issue that promotes your Mother's Day Buffet will become obsolete after Mother's Day, and you will not be taking advantage of the magazine's life span. If you use magazine advertising, your spot must feature a promotion that will not become quickly dated; otherwise, you will be wasting your money.

Magazines today are targeted very specifically. If you decide to use magazines, make sure that the readers of the magazines are in your target market. Also, make sure that you can take advantage of the entire circulation the magazine reaches. City magazines or local editions of national magazines are often good choices for restaurant ads. Specialty magazines can also be effective. For example, health clubs and golf clubs often publish their own monthly or quarterly magazines. If a significant number of your customers belong to these clubs, this could be a good way to target them. Check with your customers to determine whether they subscribe to and/or read any of the magazines in which you are thinking about advertising.

Magazines require a relatively long lead time for ad placement. Sometimes this can be four or more months in advance of the cover date. Magazines can be an effective medium if they reach your target market and most of the circulation is in your trading area.

Radio and Television Radio and television are the most common types of broadcast media. People listen to radio in their cars while they commute back and forth to work, which is why "drive time" is the most expensive time to advertise on radio stations. The prices for morning and evening drive-time ads are usually the same.

One of the principles of advertising is to advertise when people are ready to buy. If you operate a dinner house, you should advertise during the evening drive time. Messages during the morning drive time will fall on deaf ears, as drivers are typically focused on the workday ahead, rather than that evening's entertainment.

The type of audience a radio station attracts is related to the music, news, and/or talk shows it offers. Before you purchase radio space, ask your customers which radio stations they listen to.

Television provides the advantage of being able to offer people a tour of your restaurant, giving them a sense of its atmosphere. Television spots can also be used to create unique messages about your products that would be hard to do with other media. Bennigan's once ran an ad that created the image of a casual restaurant where friends could get together and have good times. The visual images of the people interacting at the table would have been hard to create in another medium.

The audience you reach in television depends on who is watching the show when the advertisement is shown. You need to know your target market and what type of shows they watch.

Television ads are expensive to produce, and airing the spots can be likewise expensive. This is why these types of ads are used primarily by national chains, local restaurant companies that have multiple units in a metropolitan area, or unique specialty restaurants that can draw from a large geographic area.

The Internet The Internet offers many additional options that can replace traditional advertising media. For instance, instead of advertising on television, you might consider adopting the video technology that real estate agents use to market homes on the Web. Another option is to join online directory services that offer streaming video-on-demand (VOD) technology. Or you might shun all other advertising media in favor of your own Web site (see Chapter 10).

Sales Promotions Sales promotions are designed to create immediate sales. They are typically used to generate sales during downtimes. They are often communicated through advertising.

> **SALES PROMOTIONS**
> Designed to create immediate sales, typically used to generate sales during downtimes, often communicated through advertising.

Popular sales promotion tools are coupons, premiums, special prices on meals or menu items, loyalty programs, contests, and point-of-purchase (POP) promotions.

As in other forms of communication, sales promotions should enhance your position. They should not confuse your guests or cause them to do the opposite of what you want them to do. For instance, if a fast-food chain targeting families wants to increase the number of children visiting its restaurants during a slow month, giving away toys in a kid's meal will attract children, whereas a special price may be ignored by both the children and their parents.

Another way to enhance your position is to link up with another business that has the same target market as you. For example, the Palm, an upscale steak house, developed a promotion in conjunction with a luxury car dealer. People who test-drove a car at this dealership were given a coupon for the Palm. The Palm sold the coupons to the car dealer for half the face value. The dealership gained a promotional tool, and the Palm gained the car dealer's customers at a low cost per table. And since many of these well-heeled customers brought guests with them, the Palm ended up with a tidy profit from this promotion.

Other upscale chains have partnered with Diner's Club or American Express to run promotions. The prestige of these credit cards serves to enhance the reputations of the chains.

There is no more immediate sale than the impulse sale. People who buy impulsively are typically the most profitable customers. Point-of-purchase (POP) displays, such as table tents, posters, and electronic sign boards within the guests' line of sight are some of the most effective ways to create this type of customer behavior. For example, Buffalo Wild Wings Grill & Bar developed a unique POP display that targeted 18- to 35-year-olds. The display, a cowboy eating a Western Burger while an armadillo sinks its teeth into him, included the line "Take a perfect break from a tough day." The promotion was developed to help the restaurant build a reputation for menu items other than its wings. The POP promotion increased sales of burgers by over 100 percent, from 2,100 to 5,000. (See Chapter 8 for other POP suggestions.)

The gift certificate is one of the best promotions you can use. Many people will buy them to give as gifts to their friends. Think about it: they are paying you to help you create new customers. They are actually paying you to help you market your restaurant. It doesn't get any better than that!

Fifteen years ago, TGI Friday's restaurants advertised gift certificates as a solution to holiday shopping. What a great idea: have a couple of beers at Friday's and do your shopping at the same time. This is exactly what Friday's was promoting—an end to parking hassles, slugging it out with other customers in the shopping malls, trying to figure out what to buy, and keeping track of how much is spent on gifts. What better way to say "Happy Holidays" to friends than to give them gift certificates to a favorite restaurant?

These days, many restaurants promote gift certificates during holiday periods. Customers expect to see them then. As a restaurant manager, however, your job is to make customers aware that gift certificates are available throughout the year. If you have a Web site, you can make it easy for people to buy them. A few mouse clicks, and your cash register starts ringing.

Another potential bonus with gift certificates is the breakage that typically occurs. *Breakage* refers to unredeemed gift certificates or unredeemed drink tickets and meal tickets for catering events. You can expect that about 20 to 25 percent of the gift certificates you sell will never get redeemed. Be aware, though, that in some states you cannot put an expiration date on gift certificates. They can be redeemed at any time. Eventually you would be allowed to write them off, but it's best to check local laws before you spend any windfall.

Premiums are items that are offered at a low cost, or at no cost, as an incentive to visit a restaurant or buy a product. Fast-food restaurants will typically sell action toys with a movie tie-in, stuffed animals, and other items for a nominal amount with the purchase of a meal. Pat O'Brien's, in New Orleans, is famous for its Hurricanes. One of the reasons for the popularity of this drink is that tourists see other tourists carrying the souvenir glasses around New Orleans, and friends see them in their homes when their vacations end.

There are an endless variety of premiums. Here are some low-cost giveaways you can use to attract attention to your restaurant:

- *Money-saving certificates or coupons.* Use your computer to create attractive, eye-catching items. Those that are unusually shaped work best, as they will stand out among the piles of things the typical consumer receives every day.

- *Articles.* Submit to various publication editors a short how-to article that contains useful material related to your restaurant. You can reach thousands of potential customers for the price of a few stamps and envelopes. You can save even this little bit of money if you e-mail the finished articles.

- *How-to brochures.* People especially love freebies that can improve their lives. For instance, you could give away a free recipe guide to people visiting your restaurant.

- *Charity tie-ins.* Donate a free product or service to one or more local charities, associations, or fraternal groups to use as a raffle prize or door prize. You'll receive a lot of attention and exposure among people who purchase tickets or attend the events.

- *Bumper stickers.* Use your computer and some special labels to make bumper stickers that highlight your operation. If you can come up with a catchy phrase, so much the better.

- *Buttons.* Buy an inexpensive button-making kit (see, e.g., www.badgeaminit.com). You can make badges for any occasion and use them to support all types of promotions.

- *Caps.* You can sell these or give them away to favored customers. Your employees can wear them, too. Don't forget to wear one yourself.

- *ID plates.* The typical ones are the refrigerator magnets used by real estate agents, repair services, and so forth. These are useful if you do a lot of delivery and take-out business. Bigger ones can be placed on the back of your car or truck.

- *T-shirts.* Or offer any other sort of clothing, such as sweatshirts or jackets. As with the caps, everyone in your operation can wear them. You can give them away or sell them. You can even use them as contest prizes; the jackets are especially popular prizes. Jackets are more expensive to produce, but T-shirts are not nearly as costly. You can buy plain shirts and use a color inkjet printer, desktop publishing software, and some transfer paper to finish them off in-house.

- *Greeting cards.* Use greeting card software and some specialty paper to make personalized greeting cards. You might send out birthday cards, holiday cards, Secretary's Day cards, and so forth.

- *Fax-on-demand.* Tell customers you will help them set up this system. Anyone with a fax machine can get information about your menus, specials, services, or anything else related to your business. Offer to give them some free paper to stock their fax machines.

- *Instant messaging.* This is basically the same as fax-on-demand. Offer to link your customers to this convenient system. Give them an incentive to join.

- *Personalized menus.* When someone is throwing, say, a surprise birthday party, offer a little more than a free piece of cake. Put out a personalized menu. Adding a couple of photos of the guest of honor, perhaps a current one and one from the past, is a nice touch.

- *Phone cards.* You can buy prepaid phone cards or create custom ones that display your name and other information. If you do this, make sure you get the kind of card that allows guests to pay for additional minutes at the same rate you paid. If it's a good rate, chances are that the guests will take advantage of it. Your name will then retain its visibility for some time.

- *Reminder stickers.* These are similar to ID plates. For example, you might make up a cute "Save Your Data" sticker that guests can place on their computer screens. They'll be reminded to back up their data, and they will see your name every time they look at the screen.

- *Posters.* Use a color inkjet printer to create appealing photos or posters of things like sunset views, forests, or beaches. Put your name on the bottom right-hand corner. Distribute them to places that might use them to dress up their walls or ceilings. Good candidates are blood banks, hospitals, dentist offices, or any other place that requires people to lie on their backs.

Contests are great sales promotions because they get people excited over a longer period of time. Unlike with many one-time promotions, the buzz contests create can last a long time. You can get a lot of mileage out of them.

Contests can take many forms. Fast-food restaurants often have sophisticated contests in which contestants can win instant prizes or collect contest pieces to form a word or fill in a series. The McDonald's Monopoly game is a good example of this type of contest.

To be worthwhile, contests must change customer behavior. They should bring new people to the restaurant or get established customers to come more often. Talking to customers or holding a focus group beforehand can tell you whether they value this type of promotion.

Focus groups we have conducted indicate that most folks prefer contests that appear to offer a reasonable chance of winning something. This is why contests that offer large cash prizes will also offer smaller prizes, prizes that seem achievable. In many contests, it's easier to be an instant winner of something small than it is to claim the top prizes. However, all instant winners should remain in the pool for the top prizes.

An instant winner might, for example, win a token that can be used to fill in a word, but can also be used to get a free or discounted sandwich. If the contest is constructed properly, people using the tokens will buy something else. If you give instant winners, say, one free taco, they will be more likely to load up on high-profit side items, especially soft drinks. Thus, you are encouraging people to buy a high-profit item when they participate in the contest.

One of the most common types of promotional contests in independent restaurants is collecting business cards and giving away two free dinners every week or every month. These business cards can be used to create a database of the restaurant's customers.

Before running a contest, make sure you understand the local laws that govern them. For example, you may be required to state the odds of winning or make the contest accessible to people who do not purchase anything. To ensure that you do not make a mistake, you might consider outsourcing the contest to a professional contest company. Not only does this keep you honest and aboveboard, but these companies are better able to maintain security, so that everyone, including you, gets a fair shake.

Contests are not just for external customers. Restaurant managers have found that contests rewarding internal customers—that is, the employees—can reduce employee turnover and make them more productive (see Chapter 7).

By far, the undisputed king of promotions is the coupon. It is also the most controversial one. Some operators won't touch them, believing that couponing tends to erode the brand image and gives people the impression that they are desperate for business. In their opinion, managers who put a "buy one, get one free" coupon in the newspaper are telling prospective customers that they have to discount prices to attract business. (See Chapter 5 for some suggested discount pricing procedures.)

Constant discounting can serve to lower a product's perceived value. For example, pizza coupons are so prevalent that many people think they are overpaying if they purchase a pizza without a coupon.

Couponing should be thought through very carefully and should not be done as a knee-jerk reaction to a bad situation. If it is done at all, it should be done as creatively as possible.

Some operators feel that, if couponing is administered properly, restaurants can boost short-term sales and create a sense of anticipation as guests await the next promotion. If you make very specific, limited-time offers that will attract new guests without giving away the store, coupons can be very effective. For instance, some restaurants give out coupons every once in a while that customers can exchange for a taster sample of a new menu item. While they're tasting, they will usually order something to go with it. If you time coupon programs to coincide with new menu rollouts, you may attract a new batch of customers, as well as encourage people to keep their eyes open for the next promotion.

One of the best ways to administer a coupon program is to use them as part of a celebration. Although the discount is important, there should be something else in the message. For example, you can develop a promotion thanking the people of your city for the support given you over the past year by providing them with a free meal when they purchase one. This sends a different message than a coupon that just says "buy one, get one free." You can celebrate your anniversary, Presidents' Day, the start of baseball season, or hundreds of other events. There are endless opportunities to turn coupons into celebrations. This creates a fun and exciting atmosphere around your restaurant.

For the most part, when using a run-of-the-mill discount coupon, you will attract price-sensitive customers without having to discount the price for everyone else. You do it just for those who bring in the coupon. Some of your customers will never use coupons; they consider them a nuisance. They are willing to pay the full price. So rather than dropping the price of all entrées by $2, place a $2-off coupon in the newspaper.

Since the aim of a promotion is to change customer behavior, track the coupon users. Are they existing customers (bad) or new customers (good)? Do any of the new customers come back without the coupon? Since those attracted to discount coupons are usually price-sensitive, many will not come back and pay full price. Therefore, you should make a profit off those using the coupon.

Some restaurants require coupon users to purchase something else. For example, Port of Subs offers a coupon for a second sandwich at half price, when the customer purchases one sandwich and two medium beverages at the regular prices. The half off attracts price-sensitive customers. The purchase of one additional sandwich and the two beverages ensures that a profit will be made from those using the coupon.

If you offer coupons, always take the time to sort through them and track the business they generate. One advantage of coupons is that you are able to do this very easily because they can be coded to help you evaluate their effectiveness. If you're putting coupons into several media outlets, you can quickly determine the effectiveness of each one.

The most creative promotion we've seen in some time, reported recently in *Nation's Restaurant News,* was a restaurant giving a 50 percent discount for "The Worst Table in the Joint." The management of Kings Family Restaurants came up with the idea of designating one table in each restaurant as the worst table. Now people come in asking for the worst table. There is only one worst table, so when it is occupied, some guests coming in for the promotion will pay full price. Is this a great promotion or what? Not only did management turn a negative into a positive, and generate a lot of buzz, it's cheap to administer since there is only one worst table.

Personal Sales

The Upper Deck seafood restaurant and supper club was open for lunch and dinner. The entertainment room, about 2,500 square feet, was quiet until happy hour started at 5 p.m. The manager,

> **PERSONAL SELLING Face-to-face guest interaction.**

wanting to make use of this space, successfully sold it for luncheons to businesses, social clubs, and charitable groups. He obtained a list of these organizations from the local chamber of commerce, contacted them, set up sales appointments, catered the events, and pocketed the money.

Suzie Amer, writing in *Restaurant Business,* tells about how Jasmine Wong used personal selling to enhance her buffet restaurant's business. Her restaurant is located just outside of Washington, D.C. One day, she noticed that tour bus drivers were stopping now and again at her operation. Eventually, it dawned on her how lucrative it would be if she could get more of this action. She figured she had the space to handle a lot of busloads, and the buffet service made it easy to get them in and out. So she set out to make sales calls at all the major tourist attractions in the area. When tour buses arrived, she approached the drivers and sold them on stopping at her restaurant. Her sales pitch included information about the restaurant and a 10 percent referral fee (commission) for the drivers based on all food and beverage sales to the passengers.

The manager of an independent pizza restaurant used personal selling to help overcome his lack of brand recognition. He called on the larger offices in his trading area, promoting his products for luncheons and office parties. He was constantly out making calls during the period between lunch and dinner. Once he hit all the offices, he started all over again in order to remind everyone that he was still there, ready to handle their needs. His efforts resulted in party orders, as well as increased awareness of his restaurant.

These examples show how the tenacious operator can generate a good deal of group business. But personal selling can also spike your individual business. Every restaurant will have a set of people and organizations that can refer individual business. Tapping into this set can create a major sales force for your restaurant.

For instance, if you are located near hotels or motels, get out and call on them. Guests often ask hotel staff for insights on where to eat. Providing free dinners to key staff or putting on a reception for them can be a good way to generate leads.

If your restaurant has a unique benefit, invite the salespeople from the local convention and tourist bureau for lunch or dinner. These salespeople come in contact with meeting planners who are looking for restaurant suggestions for themselves and their clients. If they know and like your restaurant, you will get a mention.

Think about all the people in your trading area who are in a position to refer guests to your operation. Call on them. Invite them to your restaurant and ask for their help. For example, if you are located in a shopping center, shop owners or clerks at key stores in the center can generate business for you. In a trading area with a lot of tourist attractions, people who work in the attractions and shops targeting tourists can refer visitors to your restaurant.

Don't be afraid to get out and pound the pavement. A lot of restaurant folks don't get too fired up about personal selling, thinking it is something their purveyors do, not them. Often, however, it can make the difference between profit and loss. We teach our students to be especially cognizant of the power of one on one. For instance, the class groups recreating Red Lobster restaurant for its capstone educational experience will have a very meager marketing budget, but a very ambitious sales revenue target. This is by design. It forces the students to be creative. It also forces them to get out and sell, sell, sell, instead of just hanging the Red Lobster banner outside the dining room and hoping customers storm through the doors. They learn very quickly that this doesn't happen. They also learn that you tend to build this business one guest at a time.

Personal sales in restaurants involve management and customer-contact employees. Even though you, as manager, are involved quite a bit, in reality, the full-time sales force for any restaurant is its customer-contact employees. Although you need to help sell and market your business, your main responsibility in this case is to help the guest-service staff develop and hone their selling skills.

One of the unbreakable rules of selling is that you must know the product line inside and out. Don't assume that everyone knows as much as you do about your products and services. For instance, since it is difficult for servers to sell your products if they don't have product knowledge, you must see to it that they know how the food is prepared and how it tastes. This allows them to describe the food accurately and answer guests' questions with confidence.

If guests describe the type of dish or wine they want, the server can come back with a response only if he or she knows the restaurant's food. Many people are unsure about wine options. A wine suggestion from the server is often welcome.

You have to do as much as you can to provide customer-contact employees with the best possible sales support. Provide them with as much education and as many sales tools as possible. For example, liquor distributors are often happy to conduct classes for your service staff. You can help by putting a wine-of-the-month bottle on each table, along with preset wine glasses. A nice dessert tray makes it difficult for guests to say no; many of them will at least order one dessert for everyone at the table to share. Sales contests can help the staff remember that they should be selling appetizers and desserts. The host can remind guests about upcoming events as they leave. Train your staff to sell, sell, sell. And don't forget to train them in up-selling and consultative techniques (see Chapter 7).

Business cards for servers are becoming an increasingly popular promotional tool. Business cards are inexpensive and provide servers with a way to promote the restaurant when they are not at work. Servers make their money from tips. They realize that the busier the restaurant is, the more money they make. Servers are willing to promote their restaurant if you provide them with the tools. A small investment in something like business cards will help you create an effective sales force.

Make it easy for your staff to sell. Bob Southwell, a country club consultant, uses creative techniques to help his servers. For example, Bob planned a Gay Nineties night at the Houston Country Club. To help promote the event, he asked the servers to begin wearing black garters a few days before it. When customers asked about the garters, servers would tell the table about the upcoming party. This created a natural and conversational sales pitch.

Personal sales is an effective technique that can be adapted to most promotions. Whenever you can engage customers in conversation, you have an opportunity to use it. Pretty soon, customers are selling to themselves.

Database and Direct Marketing

To implement successful direct marketing, restaurants must have access to a marketing database system. A marketing database contains information about current customers and potential customers that will be useful in developing marketing programs.

> **DATABASE AND DIRECT MARKETING** Contacting many people through direct mail, the Internet, or other similar means.

Direct marketing campaigns often target recent customers, encouraging them to return. They also are frequently used to offer incentives to repeat patrons (loyal customers) to visit during soft periods.

In *Strategic Database Marketing,* Jackson and Wang pose this question: "If you were a customer, why would you want to be on your database?" Before implementing direct marketing, you should be able to answer this question satisfactorily. You must clearly define how the guest benefits by being a part of your database.

Mail is the most common form of direct marketing. Most of us receive junk mail because those sending us the direct-mail pieces have not answered Jackson and Wang's question. Some merchants just blanket the market with mail and count on 1 or 2 percent of the recipients to respond. These national merchants don't seem to care if they irritate people, so long as one or two out of every hundred buy something.

Restaurants can't afford to have this cavalier attitude. It is dangerous to intentionally irritate guests. Customers may take abuse from, say, a department store, because they have no alternative to eventually going there to buy something. But there are too many restaurant options. You may have been their hero at lunch, but if you bug them, you'll be a bum before the dinner hour rolls around.

Restaurants are also different from mail-order houses in that they are geographically restricted. Restaurants need to create excitement with their promotions. Consider: What benefit does this mailing have for the recipients? How might the promotion change the customer's behavior in a way that benefits the restaurant, while at the same time benefiting the customer? What type of guest is most likely to view the direct approach as a positive message?

Ideally, restaurants will develop direct marketing campaigns that have more than casual appeal to their customers. For example, people purchasing fine wine could be invited to attend a special wine and food pairing dinner. Those who do not order wine or who exhibit price-sensitive behavior should not receive an invitation to this event because they would consider it junk mail.

Sending out a blanket coupon mailer for lunch Monday through Friday has little value for someone who works in another geographic area and cannot come to the restaurant for lunch. If you do a mailer, try to eliminate these folks from your database, or at least include something else they might like.

The more you know about your customers, the more value you can create with your direct marketing. If you have only names and addresses, you might promote a few different products so there is likely to be something of interest to the person who receives the direct mail. A targeted piece is preferable, but the multiple-offer method will create value when you do not have specific information about your customers.

Charlotte Bogardus, a former marketing executive for Starbucks Coffee Company, noticed that a good part of the restaurant industry was not utilizing databases to manage customer relationships. After working as a marketing consultant for Bruegger's Bagel Bakeries, Applebee's Neighborhood Restaurants, and other foodservice operations, she decided to start a company that would enable the foodservice industry to use these customer data effectively. Her company, Gazelle Systems, offers data collection, data warehousing, and knowledge management tools specifically designed to fit the needs of the foodservice industry.

Gazelle Systems uses *reverse appending,* a process of matching credit card and debit card records with demographic data (such as addresses) and psychographic information. About 60 percent of customers can be identified through reverse appending. To protect the customer's privacy, only purchases at the restaurant are reported. The information is used to develop customer profiles and high-yield, one-on-one marketing programs.

Louise's Trattoria, a chain of Italian restaurants located mostly in California, hired Gazelle Systems, which defined the restaurant's customers as "often female, interested in a healthy lifestyle, fine wines, foreign travel, and likely to try new things on the menu." Based on this profile, Louise's remodeled its restaurants, giving them a more contemporary look. The company also dropped half of the existing menu items and added more eclectic ones. One of the items they added, barbecued chicken on chopped salad, became a surprise best-seller. When analyzing the guest churn report, Louise's noticed that two of its restaurants had almost all repeat customers; the restaurants were not attracting new customers. As a result, the company developed direct marketing campaigns intended to encourage new customers to make trial visits.

TIPS FOR SUCCESSFUL DIRECT MARKETING

- A good mailing list is the most important element in a direct marketing campaign.

- Mail to customers you think will respond. A rule of thumb: Customers who came to your restaurant **R**ecently, come **F**requently, and spend more **M**oney than your average customers, are the best candidates. (Database marketing gurus refer to them as your "**RFM**" customers.)

- Make sure the offer is interesting to your target market. You should check with a few current customers to test their reactions before initiating the campaign.

- If you're undecided about which way to go, and if you have several options, put them to the test. If, for example, you cannot decide whether to give a $5-off coupon when two entrées are purchased, or a "buy one, get one free" coupon, send out a few of each and see which one provides the best return. If some customers complain that they got a lower-value coupon than their friends, always give them the higher-value coupon.

Loyalty Marketing

Database marketing is the foundation of loyalty marketing. The objective of this marketing strategy is to turn every customer into a repeat patron. As Adam Carmer, owner of Freakin' Frog Beer & Wine Cafe in Las Vegas, likes to say, the best customer is a repeat customer.

> **LOYALTY MARKETING A marketing strategy that aims to turn every customer into a repeat patron.**

Harvard researchers discovered through one of their studies that a 5 percent increase in repeat business would generate a profit increase of somewhere between 25 and 125 percent. Studies of this type illustrate the importance of repeat customers.

Repeat customers produce significant value for several reasons. They come back frequently. They purchase more when they come in. They spread positive word of mouth. They will tell you when they have a problem and give you a chance to fix it instead of just walking out and never coming back. And they are easier to serve since they know your menu and operation.

Loyal customers are customers who exhibit the behaviors you desire. They come to the restaurant on a regular basis and have positive feelings about it.

You build a loyal customer base by providing good food, service, and value. Recognition is also important. An effective loyalty program recognizes good customers and thanks them for their patronage. This recognition might take the form of a bottle of wine on their birthday or a special offer based on their dining habits.

Some chains, such as Chili's and TGI Friday's, have formal loyalty programs, similar to hotel and airline loyalty programs. Other restaurants use credit card and debit card information to gain information about their guests.

Like other promotional tools, loyalty programs should be designed to change behavior. Judd Goldfeder, president of Customer Connections, a firm specializing in restaurant loyalty programs, develops programs that stress behavior changes. When a customer's loyalty card is swiped, the computer analyzes past behavior and suggests an appropriate incentive. For example, if a customer comes in on average once every four weeks, he or she may receive a coupon that expires in two weeks, encouraging the guest to increase the number of visits.

Loyalty programs that do not recognize the customer and/or do not encourage behavior change have limited value. A program that merely keeps score isn't very useful in the long run. For example, if you go to the car wash and it gives you your tenth wash free, it doesn't add much to the car wash operator's bottom line. After all, if you like the car wash, you're going to go there no matter what. If you don't like it, you'll never go back after the first time. Yet you see all kinds of loyalty cards that give the customer the tenth (fill in the blank) free. All you're doing in this case is giving away something people are already willing to pay for. This might work for generic products, such as gasoline, where customers exhibit less brand loyalty, but it would be the rare restaurant that could benefit from this strategy.

The more sophisticated loyalty programs use considerable technology to recognize customers and encourage behavior change. For instance, a computer system can track customers' birthdays, anniversaries, what have you, and suggest appropriate recognition, such as greeting cards or a donation to their favorite charity. The options are limitless.

These types of programs can also suggest rewards that have a good chance to change a guest's behavior. For example, the computer notices that a guest never orders dessert. That would trigger a coupon for a free dessert on the next visit. If the guest tries dessert once, he or she might get in the habit and order dessert more frequently in the future.

The golden rule of loyalty programs: They should focus on recognition and changing behavior. Keeping score is for ball games.

Public Relations

Public relations involves maintaining a favorable image with all the constituencies, or "publics," with whom you interact. These publics include the community, government officials, investors, purveyors, customers, and employees.

> **PUBLIC RELATIONS**
> Maintaining a favorable image with all those with whom you interact.

Smart restaurant managers work with residents of the community and with government officials to make sure their operations are accepted in the community and that they have addressed any resident concerns. One restaurant operator fought the community and received approval to open the restaurant only because the zoning laws allowed it. However, after the restaurant opened, he had to spend thousands of dollars on marketing communications aimed at the residents he was fighting. This was futile, and his restaurant soon went out of business.

Most restaurants need the support of their communities. This starts with good public relations. A big part of public relations is publicity. Publicity is free mention of your restaurant in the media.

Publicity can be good or bad. Foodborne illness outbreaks or poor health reports printed in the local newspaper or broadcast on TV are examples of negative publicity that will cause you to lose customers. Even things that are out of your span of control can bring about the same result. For instance, a robbery at your place of business can make a lot of customers avoid your operation, at least for a while.

Good managers will eliminate most chances for negative publicity. They will also work on gaining positive publicity.

There are numerous ways for restaurants to gain good press—more so than for a lot of other types of businesses. Many people are interested in food and beverage. Publicity outlets love to include information about these things. For instance, writing a column for the local paper can be one way to keep your restaurant in front of your target market.

Creative promotions can generate positive vibes. They can lead to public relations opportunities for your restaurant. Taco Bell is a master at this.

In 2001, as the *Mir* space station was returning to earth, it was expected to scatter debris in the South Pacific Ocean, somewhere between Australia and Chile. Taco Bell floated a 1,300-square-foot vinyl raft off the coast of Australia. The raft represented a target, consisting of two circles and Taco Bell's bell logo as the bull's-eye. Around the outer circle were the words "free taco." Taco Bell promised to give everyone in the United States a free taco if a piece of the spacecraft hit the bull's-eye on the raft. It is estimated that the promotion would have cost $10 million if anything had hit the raft. Even though *Mir* didn't hit the raft, Taco Bell received international publicity for the event, worth hundreds of thousands of dollars, for a few bucks' worth of vinyl. The company probably couldn't have bought that much buzz at any price. As a precaution, though, Taco Bell purchased insurance to cover the cost in case the company had to give away millions of tacos.

Taco Bell once placed full-page ads on April Fools' Day, stating that it was helping to reduce the national debt by purchasing the Liberty Bell, which it intended to rename the Taco Liberty Bell. The controversial ad created a lot of attention. Many angry citizens called government officials, only to be reminded that it was April Fools' Day. The ad's uniqueness and the interest it created encouraged broadcast and print media coverage of the hoax. Taco Bell estimated that the ad generated over $20 million worth of publicity. Taco Bell is the master, all right.

Keeping up with what is happening in the world and in your community can uncover public relations opportunities. Barry Cohen, CEO of the Olde San Francisco Steakhouse, tells of the time when kids from his community went on what they thought would be an experience of a lifetime. A number of teenagers from San Antonio were promised jobs in the Summer Olympics if they could provide their transportation to Atlanta. Many bought one-way tickets, planning on using their earnings to fund the trip home. When they arrived in Atlanta, the jobs they were promised did not exist. This caused an outrage in the local community, which was well covered by the local news outlets. Executives at the Olde San Francisco Steakhouse arranged for Continental Airlines to bring the kids home and planned a big welcome-back party at the restaurant. The American Heart Association created special heart awards for the children to recognize their positive spirit. The party provided a happy end to their journey and was covered by local media. This event created a great deal of goodwill for the restaurant. Cohen noted that the total cost was less than the price of a large newspaper ad.

Local Area Marketing

A specialized area of public relations is local area marketing, also

> **LOCAL AREA MARKETING**
> **Marketing that concentrates on creating goodwill in a restaurant's trading area and its local community.**

called *neighborhood marketing* or *local store marketing.* This type of promotional effort is more feasible for the typical restaurant operator. After all, few operators have Taco Bell's resources.

Local area marketing concentrates on creating goodwill in a restaurant's trading area and its local community. The aforementioned reception for the Olympic workers at the Olde San Francisco Steakhouse is a good example of local area marketing. Things like this translate into increased awareness and loyalty among a restaurant's target market.

McDonald's is the parent of local area marketing. Yellow and orange jugs full of McDonald's orange drink are familiar to anyone who has children. McDonald's freely gives orange drink, cookies, toys, and even sandwiches to local charitable events. It knows that creating goodwill with the families in each store's trading area is a smart way to promote its own business.

Independent restaurants can compete effectively in local area marketing with the giants like McDonald's. In fact, locally owned and managed restaurants have an advantage because the manager is part of the community and will remain part of the community. Chain restaurants usually turn their managers every few years.

Tom Feltenstein, the guru of neighborhood marketing, states that you should be aggressive and creative when it comes to local area marketing. For example, if the firefighters ask you to be a collection site for their holiday toy drive, suggest ways of getting the drive off to a good start. For instance, you might consider kicking it off by offering a free food item or a meal discount to everyone who donates a toy on the kickoff day. The fire department should have fire engines and firefighters in uniform in your parking lot.

This will attract attention to your restaurant, but to make sure you maximize the attention, you should also call the local media, which generally love to showcase this type of thing. This local area marketing tactic will create awareness for your restaurant, as well as community goodwill.

Grade schools are always looking for nearby places to go on field trips. Why not invite the children to come out to your restaurant during a downtime in the afternoon? If you are a pizza restaurant, let them put the toppings on their own personal pizza. If you are a full-service restaurant, your chef can show them how to make a dessert. Send them home with the snack they helped to make, along

---

THINGS TO CONSIDER WHEN PLANNING A PROMOTION

- Check your product before you promote. Promotions provide a long-term return on investment and a competitive advantage only when you have good, consistent product value.

- Remember that promotions work. They will increase business. Make sure you are ready for it.

- Promotions should be designed to change behavior. Does the promotion change the behavior of the customers in a way that benefits the restaurant?

- Plan your promotions. Each promotion should fit into an overall promotional plan for your restaurant. Don't be impulsive. Avoid getting involved in promotions on the spur of the moment.

- When you purchase media placements, make sure most of the people exposed to those media are part of your target market.

- Prepare a budget, and make sure the promotion will give you a positive return on investment.

- Evaluate the promotion's results. Use what you learned to make your next promotion more successful.

- Create synergy by using all of the promotional tools.

with a coupon redeemable when they bring their parents to the restaurant.

Some restaurants work with schools and nonprofit organizations for fundraisers. One option is to give the organization 10 percent of the sales made to guests who present a flyer given out by the organization. The restaurant gains the promotional efforts of the organization, pays for only the sales that were created, and gains the organization's goodwill.

Here are some good examples of this type of promotion. A high school band meets once a month at Baja Fresh. The restaurant gains $500 worth of extra business on these nights, and the band gains a nice social event and $50 every month for its treasury. Applebee's and McDonald's give students free food or meals for making good grades. A student who gets a card for a free kid's meal because she made all As and Bs is going to be proud of her gift and make sure her parents help her take advantage of it. So the free kid's meal creates goodwill and results in the sale of one or two adult meals. Jackpot Hotel and Casino, in Jackpot, Nevada, once allowed the local school to hold its cake sale in the lobby. The hotel/casino's customers were pleasantly surprised to see this. Although there wasn't a way to trace any increase in business to this event, chances are that people are still talking about it (well, at least we are).

Bob Krummet, in *Restaurant Hospitality,* describes how Tom Kee, chef at the Rail Stop restaurant, designed a creative and fun program for children. The kids spent the Saturday before Mother's Day at the restaurant. They learned how to set a table and make brownies. Kee made arrangements with the ceramic shop next door to let the kids finish the day by making a special ceramic plate for their mothers. The program created goodwill, strengthened a good working relationship between the restaurant and neighboring businesses, and gained publicity for the Rail Stop. Furthermore, it drove extra business to the restaurant. For the kids' families coming to the restaurant on Mother's Day, Kee arranged to have Mom's dinner served on the plate made by her child, creating a memory the mother will never forget.

The ways to get involved in local area marketing are endless. You or your chef can write a food or wine column for the local newspaper, offer to be a speaker for local clubs, designate a portion of your parking lot as the site of a car wash (all the promotional material for the car wash should have your name on it), or teach cooking courses for your local college's continuing education program.

This list is limited only by your imagination and the imaginations of those with whom you discuss potential opportunities. For example, a supper club in Dallas provided transportation to the Dallas Cowboys home games at cost. The club served refreshments during the 40-minute ride. When the busses arrived at the stadium, the guests were dropped off at the gate, avoiding a long walk through the parking lot. The fans enjoyed this service, while the restaurant enjoyed having 100 customers meeting (and spending money) at the restaurant before and after the game.

When you start brainstorming ideas on how to get your local area marketing program started, remember that it should be a win-win situation for the community and the restaurant. Choose and create events that will be beneficial to the restaurant, while at the same time benefiting your target markets or organizations associated with them.

You cannot provide support for every nonprofit organization, so think about the exposure you will get from the resources you commit. Paying $500 for a half-page ad in a program that will be seen by a handful of parents attending a class recital is not a good use of your funds. Telling the sponsors of the program that, if they hand out discount flyers to members of their organization, you will buy an ad based on the amount of revenue the organization creates is a good idea. If they say it's too late to do that this year, tell them that you will be happy to work with them next year.

Word of Mouth

Word of mouth is one of the cheapest, yet most effective, promo-

WORD OF MOUTH Customers passing along their view of a business to friends, family, and other associates.

tions. Unfortunately, it's a gate that swings both ways. While positive word of mouth can drive business, negative word of mouth can scare it away.

You have to be attuned to your customers' feelings. If they have a complaint about something, you want them to tell *you*, not their friends. You want them to give you a chance to make it right. As Don Smith used to say, "The answer is yes. What's the question?" When you can make things right, you turn a negative into a positive. Guests who feel they were treated properly and with concern are likely to return and tell their friends.

You need to create a chain reaction of positive word of mouth. When customers tell you how great the food is, or how much they love your operation, tell them you are glad they enjoyed everything and to please tell their friends about your place. Too often, managers assume that if they create an excellent product and a superb overall experience, positive word of mouth will follow. You can't fall for that type of thinking. It doesn't hurt to encourage positive word of mouth. You need to let customers know that you would appreciate it very much if they would tell their friends about your restaurant. It's up to you to plant the positive word of mouth idea in their heads; don't leave it to chance.

CREATING SYNERGY

As we've discussed, there are a number of tools you can use to promote your restaurant. In order to gain full advantage, though, you need to use as many of them as possible for each promotion you do.

Let's say you have a sports bar, and you want to do a promotion on May 11. You go to www.infoplease.com and discover that Steve

Bono, former quarterback of the Kansas City Chiefs, was born on May 11. So you decide to have a Steve Bono birthday party. A week before the party, you explain the promotion to the servers and give each one a Kansas City Chiefs baseball cap to wear. The customers are now asking your employees why they are wearing Chiefs ball caps. Personal selling has kicked in. You put up promotional material around the restaurant. Since Kansas City is known for its barbeque, you create barbeque specials based on Kansas City recipes that you can promote for the week. You create a direct-mail piece and send it to your regular customers. The recipes can be shared with local media to create some publicity for the event. Advertisements can be placed in the local media. You get the idea.

THINGS TO DO TODAY

- Make this your mantra: "I must be ready for the increased business."

- Find an outdated coupon for another restaurant. Visit the restaurant and try to use it. Judge the reaction.

- Think about having a "Best Table" promotion. How would you set it up?

---

http://tca.unlv.edu/profit

10

TECHNOLOGY: HOW DO I SURF
MY WAY TO SUCCESS?

We're bombarded with technology. Like fire, it can be our worst nightmare. But if used correctly, it can be our greatest ally. One thing's for sure: you're either on the technology bandwagon or you're headed in the wrong direction. If you're not on board, you limit your opportunities to grow and prosper.

Most places have the typical forms of technology, things that we're accustomed to seeing everywhere. We expect restaurant operators to use electronic cash registers or point-of-sale computer systems and to hire technologically sophisticated payroll processing and accounting firms. What's not so common is the restaurant operator who harnesses the power of the Internet to exploit every little marketing opportunity that comes along. Sooner or later (probably sooner), in addition to becoming the most prominent research tool, it will be a significant communication medium between you and your customers, suppliers, stockholders, and potential employees.

WORLD WIDE WEB (WWW)

The World Wide Web's advertising power is just beginning to be understood. Studies have shown that consumer acceptance of online advertising is comparable to their acceptance of traditional media and that online advertising dramatically increases advertisement awareness after only one exposure.

Online advertising is more likely to be noticed than television advertising. If your restaurant doesn't have a Web site, why not? If you have one, how effective is it?

The Web is becoming a bonanza for those perceptive enough to understand how to capitalize on this unique medium. As more and more consumers log online through their television sets, and ultrafast cable modems become more common, businesses without Web sites will be perceived as dinosaurs that are behind the times. The ease of making a Web page with Microsoft's FrontPage®, Netscape®, or any of the other pagemaking software, which eliminates the need to learn the intimidating HTML coding process, is spawning legions of Web page creators, from children to grandparents.

A recent study conducted by Scarborough Research, a New York consumer ratings firm, found out that in the nation's 64 largest metro areas, an average of 43.7 percent of adults were using the Internet. Washington, D.C., was the nation's most Internet-savvy market; 59.9 percent of its residents were online. San Francisco, Austin, Seattle, and Salt Lake City had 50 percent or more of their populations online. Rounding out the top ten metro areas surveyed were Dallas, Denver, Houston, Los Angeles, and Norfolk. Fort Lauderdale and Las Vegas were tied for 28th place, with 41.8 percent using the Internet. The nation's least Internet-savvy metro area, according to the study, was Pittsburgh; only 30.8 percent of its residents were online.

What message should we take from studies like this? It seems pretty clear: if you're not online yet, what are you waiting for? Schools and colleges today teach many things online. Young kids are so accustomed to the Internet that it's hard for them to think of any other way to do business or interact with people. If you're not on their radar screen, it's comparable to having a restaurant with an unlisted telephone number.

Some folks balk at the cost and time needed to engage in online activities, such as Web site development and maintenance. What can we say to the owner of a local, tiny operation that can't conceive of expending this type of effort? Is it really necessary for this operator to have a Web site?

The cost and benefit of a Web site are probably more in balance for the larger, full-service restaurants and any other types of restaurants that enjoy a vast trading area. For instance, an expense-account restaurant catering to the convention trade would profit from a Web site. Likewise with a restaurant that can offer customers all sorts of online purchase opportunities; for instance, the Harley-Davidson Cafe can make it very easy for customers to buy logo merchandise from the comfort of their homes.

While a Web site today is not a burning issue for the smaller neighborhood operations, sooner or later it will be as necessary as the phone and fax machine. Though it may seem unlikely today for some operators, eventually it will give them exposure that could easily turn into increased sales. For instance, with a Web site, even the small doughnut shop owner is able to communicate with a wider group of potential customers. These folks may stumble upon the site and end up purchasing something online. Or they may think about it the next time they want to buy a party tray for their holiday parties at work. By monitoring the Web site hits and capturing e-mail addresses, the owner can pinpoint inexpensive promotions to targeted audiences. The additional revenue will eventually more than make up for the cost of these online efforts.

WEB SITE DEVELOPMENT: DOs AND DON'Ts

Here are some issues to consider when planning your own Web site.

Doing It Yourself versus Outsourcing

One of the first things to decide is whether you want to build the Web site yourself or outsource the work to a professional Webmaster. If you don't have a good computer, with lots of memory, and you don't know much about the Web, you are better off hiring someone to do the work. But if you have the resources and the desire, there are continuing education courses offered at most public colleges and private technical schools that can teach you the basics of using a pagemaker.

When you create your own site, you have more control over the layout and design. You can save money by doing it yourself. Furthermore, you also can keep the whole site up-to-date more efficiently.

Layout and Content

The next logical issue to consider is the layout and the type and amount of content you should have on your Web site. Layout includes things such as how quickly graphics load and the speed at which a visitor can navigate the site. Content includes the information you wish to convey and unique features, such as interactive capabilities. It is difficult to strike the right balance between too much and too little. The best approach is to view as many Web sites as possible to get some idea of what might work best for you.

The Web site developed for this book, http://tca.unlv.edu/profit, was created on Netscape by Patti Shock, who also maintains it. She has created several sites, including the one for the William F. Harrah

College of Hotel Administration, which regularly receives unsolicited compliments. You're on the right track if you can model your site after her work.

Creating the Text

Writing for the Web is different from writing for a hard-copy publication. People don't read from a screen the same way they read from hard copy. Reading from a screen is approximately 25 percent slower than reading from paper. Computer screens show a smaller section of a document, with minimum context; it is more difficult for the eye to scan the entire document.

A solid screen of print will turn people off. People tend to scan a screen, so you need a lot of space, breaks, colors, and headlines in order to divide the information into small bites. Most people will not scroll down without some positive incentive to do so. Be concise, and use spacing to your advantage.

Check out "Writing for the Web" at www.wdvl.com/Internet/Writing/. This site provides a lot of useful advice and guidance for those who want to create and maintain their own Web sites.

Site Maintenance

If your Web site is professionally done, or you or your employees don't have the time to maintain the whole site, you should maintain at least one or two pages that can be linked to the main site. The page(s) that you maintain personally can be updated more frequently—say, weekly—and uploaded easily to the main site. This approach gives you the look of a professionally developed Web site, with the ability to keep it fresh, while simultaneously minimizing your out-of-pocket expenses.

It is important to keep your Web site fresh and current. You need to be especially vigilant to ensure that critical information, such as days and hours of operation, phone and fax numbers, expiration dates on promotions/coupons, and the names of contact persons, is up-to-date. When you do your own updating, not only can you save money, you also can get the changes done quickly; your change requests don't have to wait in line at the Web site administrator's office.

Don't think of a Web site as just another ad. An ad, once published, is static. A Web site must be dynamic. Like a newborn baby, it needs consistent and regular changing.

Attracting Repeat Visitors

It's a challenge to get customers to visit your site more than once. One way to generate this type of interest is to add lots of pictures and change them frequently. You should keep a digital camera around to take pictures of your staff, parties, decorations, customers, and so on, and upload them to the site. This gives customers a reason to revisit—especially those who might be in one of the pictures.

The Web site for Milan Restaurant, in Pine Brook, New Jersey (www.milanrestaurant.com/launch.html), makes effective use of pictures. It features a slide show that is updated regularly. This keeps customers coming back again and again.

If you can afford it, consider using videos instead of pictures. Full-motion video is the way to go, and Web cams are the best technology for this purpose. Some restaurants produce live streaming video. If you type "restaurant cam" into Google (www.google.com), lots of them will pop up.

In addition to featuring live streaming video, some restaurants have become full-blown cybercafes, offering Internet access to customers.

With Web cams, people from all over the world can log on and watch the action. As a bonus, the owners can keep an eye on the business while sitting at home or at the corporate headquarters.

Another way to create return visits is to post Internet specials, contest information, the results of surveys, breaking news, unique links, giveaways, travel tips, games, restaurant reviews, and an advice column. Advice is one of the most popular freebies on the Internet. A big advantage of offering advice is that it allows you to simultaneously demonstrate your expertise and create goodwill.

Home Page

The Web site's home page is the page where people first enter your Web site. Your home page needs to be quick and easy to load. You typically have only a few seconds to capture visitors' attention; after that time, they'll usually decide to move on. If your site's home page contains a lot of graphics and too many bells and whistles, visitors may have to wait as long as five minutes for it to download—maybe even longer if they are using slow modems. Someone has to really want to see what is on a page in order to wait that long.

Make It User-Friendly

Your site must be user-friendly. It must be easy to navigate. It's critical to test the site before putting it online. Ask some of your staff, friends, neighbors, customers, and anyone else who might have input to visit and give you critical feedback. Take the time to "shop" it yourself every once in a while. It's amazing how many Web site owners do not visit their own Web sites. If they did, maybe we wouldn't encounter so many glitches.

Clarity is important. It is vital that your Web site be clear and comprehensible. Surfers can be very impatient. They will not stick around if they get confused about the content or if the graphics take too long to download. The trick is to keep it simple, yet enticing.

The Web site must also have the critical information readily visible, not only on the home page but on all successive pages. Things such as the address, phone number, fax number, and names of contact persons need to be highly visible. We've seen sites where a visitor would have to spend a few minutes to find the name of the restaurant's catering coordinator and her direct-line phone number. We've also found ourselves on home pages that didn't even tell us the city or state where the restaurant is located.

Too many sites require visitors to take unnecessary steps to arrive at their desired place. Don't waste your visitors' time; don't force them to hunt all over to find your menu or directions to your restaurant.

Some sites have nondescriptive links that can confuse visitors. However, those whose home pages feature good, descriptive links that lead to other pages on the site sometimes fail to put additional category links on these other pages. Don't make the mistake of including only a link to your home page at the bottom of each subsequent page on your site. You should include links to each of the main sections of your Web site on every page. By doing so, your visitors can choose where they want to go next. No one wants to have to keep going backward in order to go forward.

For example, you should have a link to MapBlast (www.mapblast.com) or MapQuest (www.mapquest.com) on every page that lists your restaurant's address. This way, whenever someone clicks on the address, a map pops up.

Be sure your links go to where they say they are going. Don't make visitors click all over the place to find what they are looking for. As you increase *link density* (the number of sites linked to your site), it becomes more challenging to monitor this, because sites frequently shut down, change addresses, or become dated. Make sure your visitors don't run into these problems, because they can reflect negatively on your own Web site.

A good way to tell whether your Web site is user-friendly is to do a *reverse link lookup.* In other words, you ask a search engine to tell you how many other Web sites are linked to your site. It can be very gratifying to discover a large number of links, as it verifies the value of your Web site.

Another good way to track user-friendliness is to calculate the percentage of business you derive from the Web site. For example, you can direct visitors interested in booking a party to call "Jane" for information. Since there is no Jane employed in your operation, you know that those asking for her were directed from your Web site.

Background and Color

Your Web site should not feature garish colors and/or a background that clashes or makes it difficult for visitors to read the text. Avoid backgrounds with the .bmp extension because they take too long to load.

Multiple Sites

If you have more than one target market for your restaurant, consider creating a different site for each one and using them as backdoors to your main site. This allows you to tailor a site to a particular audience and to use different keywords with each site.

For example, some audiences use personal data assistants (PDAs), such as Palm Pilot® and Handspring®, that are more than merely electronic notepads and organizers. They are now capable of searching the Web. The wireless connections are still very slow, but if you put up a site that doesn't have too many bells and whistles, users will still be able to get the essential information quickly. In this situation, it would be best to have text-only pages, as these are easier to load. Ironically, this advancement in wireless technology has brought the Web full-circle, since the early days featured text-only pages.

Each target market is likely to search using different keywords. For example, the same large pizza operation with an attached playground/carnival area may show up for a surfer looking for pizza restaurants as well as for a surfer looking for children's entertainment. The more keywords you incorporate, the more potential business you can drum up. Try to determine the kinds of keywords potential customers are most likely to use when searching, and structure your pages accordingly.

Keywords are the means by which the search engines find your site. The search engines use robots to crawl sites looking for these keywords. However, search engines do not crawl sites that have frames. Thus, you should avoid frames on your site(s) not only because of this problem, but because frames can be confusing.

Banner Ads

When building a Web site, you may have the opportunity to participate in banner ads, those annoying little pop-ups that clutter the site and distract surfers. Though they may help defray the costs of operating your site, they tend to cheapen it. You might also consider avoiding links to your site that have them.

Domain Name

Every Web site needs a domain name. It's better to register your own domain name (e.g., www.myrestaurant.com), instead of using the domain of another server (e.g., www.accesscompany.com/ ~myrestaurant.html). Having your own domain name makes it easier to remember and creates a better image. Using another's domain may be less expensive, however. For example, some Yellow Pages offer advertisers a very limited site as part of their service and include it in the basic Yellow Pages monthly fee.

Before you go through the trouble of reserving a Web address/domain name, say it out loud, as if you were telling it to someone over the phone. How easy is it to say? Is it easy to remember? Will you have to spell it every time you say the name? Does it contain confusing hyphens or underscores? Is it case sensitive?

If your preferred name is unavailable, try a variation of it. For example, www.myrestaurantcity.com may be a good second choice.

It costs $70 to register a domain name for two years, with a $35-per-year renewal fee thereafter. Register through Internic at www.internic.net. You can choose a .com or a .net extension.

Interactivity

Avoid creating a *billboard site*—that is, a site that has only one-way communication. Interaction with potential customers is important. A link to your e-mail allows you to solicit and receive feedback, and also enables you to capture leads. For instance, you want people to be able to easily make and verify reservations, opt to join your in-house mailing list, order and pay for logo merchandise, request information, subscribe to your online newsletter, contribute to an online discussion group, or complete forms needed to process catering requests. If you offer a great deal of interactivity, though, you must answer inquiries promptly or risk alienating customers.

Interactivity allows you to capture a great deal of customer information, which can enable you to create all sorts of databases that can be used to promote your events and specials. However, you must be careful that you do not violate your customers' confidence by selling such data to third parties. To maximize the opportunity to capture customer data, place an e-mail link, location information, and phone number on each page of your Web site.

One application for customer data is to establish a customer loyalty program. You can offer good customers a free gift or discount coupon for achieving a certain level of purchases. Capturing data from these loyal folks really allows you to get to know them better. This will help you fine-tune your overall marketing effort.

Internet Service Provider

You will have to select an Internet service provider (ISP). This is the company with which your site will reside. Depending on the size of your Web site, it can cost from $25 to $50 per month. Before selecting the provider, ask for references from satisfied clients. Some providers are better than others.

Search Engines

You will need to submit your Web site to various search engines. Each search engine requires a separate submission, and it's a good idea not to limit yourself to just one or two.

If you are not on the search engines, it's unlikely that you will be found by all potential customers. To demonstrate this, go to the search engine www.dogpile.com, a multisearch engine that searches about 20 other search engines at once. Type in the word "catering." As you view the results, you will find that one engine produces approximately 10 hits, another produces about 200 hits, and yet another produces several thousand. There is a very wide variation.

What surfers find depends on the search engine they are using. Since you can't tell what they might be using, submit your site to as many search engines as possible. At www.addme.com, you can submit your Web site to a number of search engines at one time. A note of caution: Don't submit your site to the search engines until it is finished. A work-in-progress creates a negative image.

Printing

Many people like to print off Web pages. Consider how your site would look if it were printed. If someone prints only your home page, are all the vital elements available, such as hours of operation, menus with prices, phone number, fax number, address, e-mail address, and contact information?

If your Web site has frames, customers can't print the whole page, but only the center frame. This is another reason to avoid frames when designing the site.

Be wary of having a site that uses the excessive bells and whistles that require Shockwave or other, similar types of plug-ins promoted by Web page designers. Those without the latest computer equipment will not be able to view sites that are too jazzy, nor will those using text-only Internet appliances.

Promotion

Don't forget to publicize your Web site wherever and whenever you can. Put your Web site address (URL) everywhere: on your business cards, stationery, T-shirts, caps, pencils, pens, key chains, all advertisements, and so on. A Web site is only as good as the promotion you put behind it. Having a Web site without aggressive promotion to support it is like hanging your restaurant's sign in the basement.

Competitors' Web Sites

Don't get so involved in your own Web site that you ignore the others out there. Visit your competitors' sites to see what they're up to. There are bound to be several good ideas that you can borrow from them.

There are many food- and beverage-related Web sites that contain tips and ideas you can use immediately to increase your business, become more efficient, and keep up with the competition. If you want to discuss a particular marketing problem that you are trying to solve with others who understand the industry lifestyle and culture, try the discussions at Web Food Pros (www.webfoodpros. com/discuss). Epicurious (www.epicurious.com) is a fascinating site, offering recipe searches, a food glossary, and many other useful features. Many singles of all ages are uncomfortable dining out alone. If you are interested in organizing singles for group dining experiences, visit www.friendshipdining.org. Another site to bookmark is On The Rail (www.ontherail.com), which features tons of resources, newsgroups, and bulletin boards. In The Weedz (www.intheweedz. com) offers a unique slant on this crazy restaurant business. The Restaurant Report (www.restaurantreport.com) is both a Web site and a complimentary e-mail newsletter. It is an outstanding resource, made more valuable by the on-site archive of back issues.

You will often run across food and beverage sites that would be great to link to yours. For instance, Chowhound (www.chowhound. com) is an interesting site, where restaurant patrons who are serious foodies share their experiences. Sites like this can enhance your overall marketing efforts.

You also might find restaurant search sites. For example, if you join Food.com (www.food.com), Restaurant.com (www.restaurant.

com), or Menu-online (www.onlinemenus.com), the extra exposure might increase your sales revenues substantially. At Restaurant.com, guests can make reservations at over 165,000 restaurants in more than 13,000 cities. However, do keep in mind that some of these sites charge a fee.

THINGS TO DO TODAY

- Check out this book's Web site.

- Just for fun, check out www.dinersoft.com.

- Enroll in a pagemaking software continuing education class.

---

http://tca.unlv.edu/profit

11

MARKETING PLAN AND BUDGET: HOW DO I FIGURE OUT WHAT TO DO AND HOW MUCH IT WILL COST?

As they say, if you fail to plan, you plan to fail. And if you don't know where you're going, any road will take you there.

We've talked about a lot of different things in this book. But we can't stop until we say a few things about how it should all come together.

Jack Welch, former CEO of General Electric, said that if you do not have a competitive advantage, don't compete. In the restaurant business, we're more likely to put it a little differently: you're only as good as your last meal.

These statements capture the essence of why you need to develop a marketing plan. In Chapter 3, we discussed how the environment is changing and, as a result, your market is changing.

A restaurant doing well today cannot take future success for granted. It must continually adjust to environmental changes in order to pave the way for continued prosperity. Developing an annual marketing plan forces you to keep up with environmental trends. The purpose of preparing an annual marketing plan is to make sure you have a full house next month and a full house one or two years from now.

While you are developing your marketing plan, you should be constantly asking yourself: how can I create and maintain a competitive advantage? The marketing planning process forces you to look inward, to analyze your operating procedures—to realize that what worked yesterday may not work well tomorrow.

The big restaurant chains spend a great deal of time and effort developing all sorts of plans. They also tend to outsource some of this work, which is not feasible for the typical independent operator—you need to do it yourself. You may not be able to put together a beautiful document with a multimedia presentation, and you might not have the benefit of professional advisers who do this sort of thing for a living, but, in the end—if you're honest with yourself—you can develop a pertinent, useful plan that suits your needs.

A potentially huge advantage of doing this work yourself is that you are more likely to identify weaknesses in your operation. You also might be the best one to judge how serious a weakness is.

You may be able to develop a plan to minimize the impact of some weaknesses. For example, if your small kitchen is becoming more of a problem because your customers are demanding greater variety and more choices, you will need to become a more creative menu planner to accommodate guests, even though you have limited production facilities.

You may discover a weakness that is difficult to overcome. A professional consultant who picks up on this might make a suggestion that is too expensive or is otherwise not feasible. You would probably be more pragmatic and decide to avoid competing in an area that would expose your weakness to the public. For instance, if your kitchen is becoming too small, an outside consultant would be likely to suggest remodeling or retrofitting it. However, because it's your own money, you would tend to be more cautious in your own assessment, and would find a solution that is more in keeping with your existing capabilities.

So you need a **marketing plan.** It doesn't have to be elaborate, but it does need to be complete. If you touch all the bases, you will have a good handle on what must be done. You will not overlook anything. And you will get the most out of your marketing dollars.

> **MARKETING PLAN   A description of what you plan to do to fill your restaurant with happy guests.**

A restaurant marketing plan should contain sections that include or address the following:

I.   Executive summary
II.   Opportunities and threats created by environmental changes
III.   Strengths and weaknesses of the restaurant
IV.   Deciding what you want to achieve
V.   Action plans: strategies and tactics
VI.   Cost estimates
VII.   Review and update
VIII.   Information for next year's plan

EXECUTIVE SUMMARY

The executive summary allows you to quickly share the plan with assistant managers, new management employees, and anyone else who helps you promote the restaurant. If you are part of a chain, or if you are an independent that has to report to investors, the executive summary may be the only part read by these parties.

The summary should include the following content:

- Brief overview of your SWOT Analysis (see Chapter 3)
- List of next year's objectives, in quantitative terms
- Brief description of marketing strategies to meet the objectives
- Brief description of your target market(s)
- Brief description of the expected results of your action plan
- Budget summary

OPPORTUNITIES AND THREATS CREATED BY ENVIRONMENTAL CHANGES

In this section, you should note things going on in the environment that may affect your business. The environmental analysis section forces you to look outside of your organization. Before you write this section, you should spend time visiting your competitors. (You're doing this regularly anyway, right?) Based on your observations, answer the following questions:

- Who is coming to the restaurant?
- Was the restaurant full?
- Was the service attentive?
- Was the service friendly?
- Is the menu interesting?
- Is the food and beverage quality excellent?
- How do the menu prices compare to yours?
- What does this place do exceptionally well?
- What are its main deficiencies?

- What is your competitive advantage over this restaurant?

- Can you create any additional advantages, based on what you have observed?

Your visits to the competition should be combined with the environmental analysis described in Chapter 3. That analysis is designed to help you identify opportunities and threats that exist in your trading area. For example, if you operate a midscale restaurant, the trend toward customers ordering specialty bottled waters in places like yours creates an opportunity for you. If you are a quick-service restaurant, the growing public health concern about fast food is a threat, unless you modify your menu. When you conduct an environmental analysis, focus on those trends that will most likely impact your operation and require you to modify your day-to-day business procedures.

STRENGTHS AND WEAKNESSES
OF THE RESTAURANT

The next step is to look into your own organization and identify your strengths and weaknesses. You should play to your strengths. Shore up your weaknesses if they are in areas that are absolutely necessary to conduct your business profitably. In many cases, however, it is advisable to stay away from anything that might shed light on them.

For example, in the 1970s, a leading steak house chain was known for its great steaks and prime rib. In the 1980s, management noticed that people were eating less red meat and more pasta and seafood. As a result of this change in consumer behavior, they decided to add seafood and pasta to the menu. A promotional campaign to reposition the company followed the menu revision.

The result? A disaster. Why? Management failed to assess the organization's strengths and weaknesses. If someone had done an internal assessment, it would have dawned on everyone that the key food handlers in the restaurant units were professional broiler cooks. They could easily handle 24 steaks on a grill and have them all come out perfectly. But they were unable to prepare killer sauces and cook seafood properly. The seafood and pasta items at the restaurant were mediocre, while the steaks continued to be excellent. The overall perception of the restaurant fell, as customers were disappointed with the nonmeat items. The company quickly returned to its core business and developed the following position statement: "A Legend in Steaks." Even though everything worked out well in the end, the chain could have avoided its disastrous move into pasta had it done a good internal analysis of its strengths and weaknesses.

Here is a list of things you should consider when you do your internal analysis:

- Location: cost, visibility, accessibility

- Facilities: condition, atmosphere, efficiency, size

- Staff: service attitude, skills, commitment to the restaurant

- Finances: cash on hand, cash flow, overhead, ability to gain additional financing

- Customer base: Who are they? What do they want? How loyal are they?

- Menu: Is it creating guest satisfaction? How does it compare to the competition? Is it profitable?

DECIDING WHAT YOU WANT TO ACHIEVE

You must establish specific objectives in order to provide direction for the rest of your marketing plan. Good objectives are

- Measurable

- Achievable

- Appropriate to the organization's overall goals

Measurable objectives are

- Expressed in dollars or unit measurements, such as covers per day, sales revenue per available seat, or average check

- Time specific, that is, they should be achieved within a certain period of time, such as six months or one year

- Profit and/or contribution margin (CM) specific, such as an average food cost of 28 percent or an average CM of $10 per customer

It's not easy to establish objectives that meet these criteria. It is time-consuming. And to save time, there is a tendency, for example, to simply bump up last year's average CM per customer by 2 or 3 percent.

But to be meaningful, your objectives must be based on what you feel is achievable, what you think is most likely to occur. Let's say you've identified an opportunity to increase your customer count by expanding into the family market. You think you could increase your weekly cover count significantly if you do this. Therefore, your objective should be to

- Serve an additional 50 adult covers per week and 60 children's meals per week *(unit measure)*

- Within three months of adding a children's menu *(time specific)*

- With a food cost of 50 percent or less for the children's meals while maintaining your normal food cost (28 percent) for the adult meals *(CM specific)*

Often, your objectives will focus on developing additional market segments. This is understandable, since the heart of a marketing plan is the analysis and selection of target markets. It is inappropriate to assume that last year's target markets will automatically roll over to next year. Although it is normally true that the majority of target markets will remain the same, new ones appear, some drop out, and their order of priority may change over time.

Be alert to new markets. The deck reshuffles itself all the time; you can't hold the same cards forever. Of course, you can't tap new markets if you don't have the resources, but if you're aware of changes early on, perhaps you can reallocate those you have and strengthen your competitive edge.

ACTION PLANS: STRATEGIES AND TACTICS

When developing objectives, you should simultaneously be developing your action plans. Managers usually switch back and forth between the development of objectives and the development of action plans as they refine their marketing plans. They usually start with some objectives, then develop strategies and tactics (i.e., **action plans**) to achieve them. The process of working out the details of strategies and tactics often leads to modification of the objectives. The development of a marketing plan is an evolutionary process; it is not sequential.

ACTION PLANS Strategies and tactics developed to achieve marketing objectives.

Marketing strategies are designed to be the vehicle used to achieve your marketing objectives. Marketing tactics are the specific tools used to support the strategies. Marketing strategies and tactics employ all aspects of the marketing mix.

You need to focus on your objectives when developing these strategies and tactics. You don't want to put together an action plan that lacks direction. You can't afford to waste your time and effort.

You also need to think outside the box when doing this work. You should consider unique, creative ideas as much as possible. Furthermore, you must stay away from the types of mistakes that prevent you from developing an effective plan and achieving your objectives.

The most common mistakes managers make when developing marketing strategies and tactics, outlined in *Marketing for Hospitality and Tourism*, are as follows:

- **Desire to maintain status quo.** Some owners and managers are arrogant—a common malady in our business. They feel that things under their control are going well, so why change? If things are not broken, why should they be fixed? Unfortunately, in the fast-paced restaurant business, by the time the product is demonstrably broken, it's usually beyond repair.

- **Unsure management.** These managers do not want to take the risks that accompany changes. Eventually, their restaurants will go into decline because they have not kept up with current trends.

- **Failure to engage in marketing planning** or to view the process as being a serious and meaningful part of decision making. These managers do not make marketing plans. Their businesses often lose focus and, over time, become less competitive.

The importance of developing marketing strategies is supported by a study conducted by West and Olsen, published in the *Cornell Hotel and Restaurant Administration Quarterly.* These researchers found that restaurants possessing no specific strategy cannot expect to enjoy long-run successful performance. They may enjoy excellent returns for a number of years, but, at some point, their lack of strategy will cause the business to fail. When they begin to experience the consequences of this lack of strategic direction, it may be too late to mount an effective alternative. They concluded that, in order to be successful in the long run, restaurant managers need to develop individualized, unique strategies and tactics.

Here are some particularly good examples of successful marketing strategies and tactics:

- Panda Express wanted to strengthen its position in the family market and gain a higher average check from families. In *Nation's Restaurant News,* Amy Spector explains how Panda Express developed a tactic to support this strategy. The tactic was a new kid's meal. Management believed that this kid's meal would help make the restaurant more attractive to children. It would also increase the average check for families, since many parents did not buy separate meals for their children, but shared their food with them. As a result of this tactic, the parents and their children would each have their own dishes.

- The Flying Saucer Emporium developed a series of promotional events to give it a competitive advantage. In *Restaurant Business,* James Scarpa describes some of the tactics the company used to implement this strategy. One of them was a daily fire sale, featuring either a new beer being introduced to the market or a seasonal beer for $2.50 a pint, instead of the normal price of $4. This daily feature added excitement, since the customers did not know what was going to be on special. It also gave beer lovers a chance to taste a variety of beers. The Flying Saucer Emporium also has a club that patrons pay $14 to join. For their money, they receive a T-shirt and a magnetic card that keeps track of the beers they drink. After they sample 200 beers, they get their names placed on a saucer displayed in the restaurant's ring of honor. This promotion generates extra sales revenue and builds brand loyalty.

- The Upper Deck seafood restaurant and supper club had a strategic objective of building sales during the slow summer months. The manager developed an all-you-can-eat shrimp peel, held monthly during the summer in the entertainment room and on the outside patio. The promotion generated record sales on the days it was held. It also created residual business because of positive word of mouth by customers.

- Taco Time, a quick-service restaurant, developed a strategy to give its restaurants a more authentic feel. One of the tactics used to accomplish this was introducing a new concept, the Taco Time Cantina. According to Lisa D'Innocenzo, in an article in *Strategy,* focus groups told Taco Time's management they wanted to see their food being prepared. Customers said being handed a taco wrapped in a piece of paper was not authentic. Taco Time's management redesigned the restaurant so that the food was prepared in full view of the guests. Designers used wood accents to give the restaurant a Mexican cantina look, and they complemented the décor with Mexican music. The cantina also gives customers the option of having beer or wine with their meals.

One of the most useful tools for the action plan section of a restaurant's marketing plan is the wall calendar. A monthly calendar, including the actions needed to implement your plan and the outcomes of those actions, is essential. Your calendar should include things such as:

- Dates and times of promotional events
- Media placement, showing when communications will be running in newspapers, television, radio, or other media

- National and state holidays

- Local events, such as fairs and festivals, that may affect your business

- Paydays of large employers, if a good portion of your target market works for the same employer

- Dates on which actions must be taken to implement your plan, such as deadlines for submitting advertisements to the newspaper or the schedule of employee training sessions

The calendar enables you to see at a glance what is going on. It helps in several other ways as well. For instance, it will ensure that your promotions generate business only when it is needed, rather than when you're already flush. The calendar should be reviewed monthly and quarterly so that you always have a good feel for what is coming up.

Strategies and tactics should be developed to meet your marketing objectives. They should be based on sound marketing ideas suggested by your SWOT Analysis. Your marketing actions should be designed to give you a competitive advantage and produce a profit.

COST ESTIMATES

One of the hardest marketing decisions facing companies is how much to spend on promotion. John Wanamaker, the department store magnate, once said, "I know that half of my advertising is wasted, but I don't know which half. I spent $2 million for advertising, and I don't know if that is half enough or twice too much."

A well-developed and well-executed restaurant marketing plan does not require a large budget. Pam Felix, owner of the California Tortilla restaurant in Bethesda, Maryland, realizes that most independent operators like her don't have much of an ad budget. So she bases her promotions on inexpensive, humorous gags. Gregg Cebrzynski quotes her in a story in *Nation's Restaurant News:* "[T]he goofier we are, the more money we make." She gets her messages across through her *Taco Talk* newsletter.

Here are two examples of inexpensive, successful promotions she's used. On Jungle Noise Day, everyone who came in and made a noise like Tarzan received free chips and salsa. There is a lack of parking in Bethesda, so lots of people get parking tickets. Customers who come in with a parking ticket in hand receive a free taco. Pam uses these wacky promotions to create a fun atmosphere and also as her way of giving something back to her customers.

Many managers try to find out from their competition how much they are spending on marketing, or they try to find industry expense surveys that include what the average restaurant spends on marketing. They then try to copy the average expense in their operations. It's tempting to use this method, because it's an easy way of preparing a marketing budget. It's also reassuring; they feel they're spending the right amount, since it mirrors their competitors' budgets.

But it is not a good idea to mimic the competition or use industry averages to calculate your marketing budget. Each restaurant has unique objectives. Thus, having common expenditures does not make sense; expenses should be related to your objectives.

A well-established restaurant that consistently provides excellent food and service may spend only 1 percent of its sales revenue on marketing. The positive word of mouth generated by its reputation ensures a constant supply of new customers. It doesn't have to spend a lot of money on marketing, because promotions are needed only to enhance business during slow periods. A new restaurant, however, may need to spend 15 to 20 percent of its sales revenue on marketing during the first year in order to gain market penetration.

A marketing budget can be any amount of money. It's not a question of being too little or too much. The main issue is whether you can get back more than you spend. Who cares how much you spend, so long as you get back more? You're liable to miss this concept if you focus too much on industry averages and what competitors are spending.

The best way to determine your marketing budget is to, first, take a look at what you need to accomplish. Then, go ahead and develop a tactical plan to accomplish your objectives. Finally, cost out the plan.

Use the **"objective and task" method of budgeting** to cost out your plan. This makes it easy to justify your expenditures, because it forces you to develop a solid tactical plan and pinpoint your objectives. It also forces you to link each expenditure to the accomplishment of some objective. Furthermore, you have to show specifically how each expenditure helps you achieve each objective. In the end, you wind up with a good budget. And, given all the thought you have to put into this process, you also wind up with a specific, clear-cut plan.

> **"OBJECTIVE AND TASK" METHOD OF BUDGETING** A method of budgeting that requires developing a solid tactical plan, pinpointing objectives, and detailing how each expense is connected to an objective.

CAUTION

You cannot use the "objective and task" method of budgeting unless you have measurable objectives.

Now the guessing game begins. You know what you have to spend, but you don't know for sure how much you'll earn back. If you think that achieving the plan's objectives will generate enough money to cover its expenses, plus give you a fair profit, then the plan is justified. If you think the plan will not yield a positive return, one option is to dump it. Alternatively, you might reevaluate it to see whether there is a more cost-effective way of achieving your objectives. If you think the return isn't there, you need to go back to the drawing board.

Ideally, you would keep a file for each promotional objective. The file should contain an overview of the objective, the tactical plan used to implement it, the budgeted expenses, and the actual cost you ended up paying to carry out the plan. The results of the plan should be included with an overview of what happened, including the sales and profits generated by the plan. The file should also include your comments about what went wrong and what went right. This will provide valuable information when you develop future plans.

REVIEW AND UPDATE

No matter how much planning you do, it is very difficult to develop the perfect marketing plan. Market conditions change, disasters occur, all sorts of things crop up unexpectedly. There are times when you might spend more time revising a plan than creating it in the first place.

Marketing plans should be reviewed at least once a quarter. If there's a hitch somewhere, you need to find out what's going wrong. If you uncover a speed bump, an implementation problem is typically your troublemaker.

An implementation problem occurs when the plan was not properly implemented. For example, your marketing plan says you

---

THINGS TO DO TODAY

- Cost out a hypothetical two-for-one promotion. Do you think you could generate enough sales revenue to make it work?

- Visit your local Small Business Administration (SBA) office. Pick up the pamphlets dealing with the marketing function—and be sure to read them.

- Review a promotion that you ran in the past. Were your objectives expressed in dollars or units? Were they time specific? Were they profit and/or CM specific?

will develop a special promotion each week in order to build traffic on Tuesday night. However, you keep repeating the same promotion. It's getting dull and repetitive. As the kids say today, "It's *so* last month." Thus, Tuesday sales remain anemic.

Another common problem is overspending your budget. For example, you budgeted for a six-column-inch newspaper ad, but a newspaper salesperson convinced you that a ten-column-inch ad would be a better value. However, the bigger ad didn't create enough sales revenue to cover the additional cost. While it's great to get a quantity discount, keep in mind that, when you buy promotions, it's not the same as buying large quantities of frozen fish. You don't get the same benefit. No matter what you pay for a promotion, it's too much if it doesn't spike your sales.

In some cases, your marketing plan may be faulty from the be-ginning. This usually occurs when your environmental forecast is flawed. For example, you may not have taken into account a slow-down in the local economy and the subsequent drop in the average check. Having failed to do this, you are not in a position to adjust your marketing plan to meet this new threat. You're not ready to, for example, introduce a few inexpensive menu items to keep guests coming in, while simultaneously meeting the contribution margin (CM) requirements for your restaurant.

Reviewing your marketing plan on a quarterly basis allows you to make adjustments during the year. It also enables you to make ad-justments quickly, before too much damage is done. You don't have to wait until you develop next year's plan to correct mistakes.

THINGS TO DO TONIGHT

- Pat yourself on the back for having the patience to plow through this book.

- Congratulate yourself for understanding the importance of this book.

- Celebrate with someone you care about.

INFORMATION FOR NEXT YEAR'S PLAN

You should set aside a slow period to sit down and develop the marketing plan. For most of us, off-seasons are February and July. These are good times to get fired up for the next "silly season."

Though you will set aside a specific chunk of time each year to do the annual things, such as planning, environmental scanning, and budgeting, the process of adding information to the database needed to do a good job should be ongoing.

Use the methods described in Chapters 3, 4, and 7 to gather marketing data on a regular basis. File these data away—they will come in handy. Some of this information can be used to adjust your current marketing plan, but much of it will be used to develop next year's plan.

Your marketing plan is a work in progress that helps keep your restaurant current and profitable. The process of creating and refining it is a never-ending battle—and a never-ending satisfaction.

Ready, set, market!

THINGS TO DO TOMORROW

- E-mail one of the authors of this book—Patti Shock (shock@unlv.edu), John Bowen (jbowen@uh.edu), or John Stefanelli (stefan@ccmail.nevada.edu). Let us know what you think about it.

- Pass along your copy of this book to anyone you think would enjoy it. (Or, better for us, keep your copy and ask them to buy their own.)

---

http://tca.unlv.edu/profit

RESOURCES

The following are excellent periodicals, which are free to qualified foodservice owners and managers.

Hotel F&B Executive is addressed to foodservice managers in hotels. But many of the ideas presented are applicable to non-hotel food and beverage operations. You can subscribe by faxing a request to (847) 836-7635. You can also subscribe on the journal's Web site at www.hfbexecutive.com.

Restaurant Business is a journal for restaurant owners and managers, with an emphasis on multiunit operations; however, it is useful for independent restaurant managers, who can gain insights by checking out what the chains are doing to achieve success. The journal is divided into easy-to-read headings, with a new topic every few pages. You can reach *Restaurant Business* by mail at P.O. Box 5166, Pittsfield, MA 01203-9307, by fax at (413) 637-4343, or online at www.foodservicetoday.com.

Restaurant Hospitality is a journal for restaurant operators, executive chefs, and other decision makers in the restaurant hospitality industry. A unique feature of this journal is the editorial segment, where, each month, the editor-in-chief addresses a major issue facing the industry, which is great for environmental scanning buffs. The journal also features menu trends rather than simply individual recipes. You can reach its headquarters at 1300 E. Ninth St., Cleveland, OH 44114-1503, by phone at (216) 696-7000, by fax at (216) 696-0836, or online at www.foodservicesearch.com/restauranthospitality/index.cfm.

Restaurant Marketing includes a wealth of ideas and strategies that can help make your restaurant stand out. You can reach the journal by phone at (800) 247-3881, by fax at (662) 236-5541, online at www.restaurant-marketing.net, or via e-mail to rm@restaurant-marketing.net.

Restaurants and Institutions is a journal for foodservice operators and chefs. As the name indicates, this journal covers both commercial and noncommercial foodservice operations. Contact the magazine at P.O. Box 7589, Highlands Ranch, CO 80163, by fax at (800) 334-2812, or online at www.rimag.com.

OTHER PERIODICALS

Here are three excellent periodicals, but you have to pay to get them:

Cornell Hotel and Restaurant Administration Quarterly is a research-based journal that focuses on studies relevant to the hospitality and travel industry. You can contact it care of Elsevier Science Publishers, Madison Square Station, P.O. Box 882, New York, NY 10160-0206. The *Quarterly* maintains a Web site at www. hotelschool.cornell.edu/publications.

Nation's Restaurant News is an all-encompassing weekly newspaper that addresses just about every aspect of the foodservice industry. The articles are timely and pertinent, well suited for restaurant owners and operators, chefs, employees, or those studying the foodservice industry. It touches on just about anything and everything that you need to know. There are always several articles devoted to marketing. Also included in this tabloid are an events calendar, a product showcase segment, an advertiser index, and financial information. *Nation's Restaurant News* can be reached by phone at (800) 944-4676 or online at www.nrn.com.

Restaurants USA is a journal for restaurant owners and managers, featuring the results of research sponsored by the National Restaurant Association (NRA). This journal is an excellent source of information for trend analysis. It is free for NRA members. Nonmembers can subscribe for $125 a year. You can reach *Restaurants USA* at 1200 Seventeenth Street NW, Washington, DC 20036-3097, by phone at (202) 331-5900, or online at www. restaurant.org.

BOOKS

Here are a few excellent books you should have in your professional library. They can be ordered through our Web site (http://tca.unlv. edu/profit), where you will also find information about the books, including reviews, tables of contents, and prices.

Beverage Biz Is Show Biz!, by Dave Steadman (Spirited Living, 1999). This book is full of ideas you can use to market beverage products.

Many of the ideas come from the nation's most successful bars and restaurants.

A Complaint Is a Gift, by Janelle Barlow and Claus Moller (Berrett-Koehler Publishers, 1996). Your most loyal customers are the ones who complain, yet operators often view complaining customers as an annoyance. This book tells why you should regard complaints as gifts in disguise. It also shows you how to capitalize on the information provided.

The Experience Economy, by B. Joseph Pine II and James H. Gilmore (Harvard Business School Press, 1999). This book contains lots of ideas that you can use to create memorable and entertaining guest experiences.

Grassroots Marketing for the Restaurant Industry, by Adam Barringer (Writers Club Press, 2002). Barringer draws on his years of experience in the restaurant industry to provide marketing ideas that you can implement easily in your own restaurant.

Guest-Based Marketing, by Bill Marvin (John Wiley & Sons, Inc., 1997). A popular and highly respected restaurant consultant, Bill "The Restaurant Doctor" Marvin offers an abundance of suggestions for promoting your restaurant.

Managing the Guest Experience, by Robert C. Ford and Cherrill P. Heaton (Delmar/Thomson Learning, 2000). This book focuses on things you can do to ensure that your guests have a great experience at your restaurant. Ford and Heaton take a unique approach, discussing how to do this by managing your customers, as well as your employees.

Marketing for Hospitality and Tourism (third edition), by Philip Kotler, John Bowen, and James Makens (Prentice Hall, 2003). This is a comprehensive marketing textbook, providing a useful overview of marketing applications for the hospitality industry. It is the most popular, best-selling hospitality marketing text, and is a good read for those who want to study this activity from a variety of perspectives.

On-Premise Catering, by Patti Shock and John Stefanelli (John Wiley & Sons, Inc., 2001). This is a great resource for food and beverage managers who have function space to sell. If you want to get started in the catering business, this book will tell you how. If you are already in the catering business, this book will provide tips to make you more successful.

Restaurant Biz Is Show Biz!, by Dave Steadman (Whittier Green, 1991). Although this book is over ten years old, many of the promotions discussed are just as effective today as they were then. The format is similar to that of Steadman's companion beverage book (see above).

Restaurant Profits Through Advertising and Promotion: The Indispensable Plan, by Tom Feltenstein (CBI, 1983). Feltenstein is the master of neighborhood marketing. Most of the concepts presented in this book are still applicable today.

Service America!, by Karl Albrecht and Ron Zemke (Dow Jones-Irwin, 1985).This was one of the first books to suggest that organizations should be customer focused. Many of the ideas presented here have since become the foundation for several of the company employee-training programs that are used today.

W.O.W. 2000, by Barry M. Cohen (Savannah Corp., 1997). This book explains how to turn employees into owners. Cohen shows you how motivated employees can become your best marketers. President of Olde San Francisco Steak House, he shares things he's learned over the years that have made him the successful manager he is today.

INDEX